D0559127

Simpson

CHRISTIAN
Living

It's who you know

MAR. 1 1 2001	DATE DUE		

Bethany Baptist Church
2353 E. GRAND BLANC ROAD
GRAND BLANC, MICH. 48439
PHONE 694-88

IT'S WHO YOU KNOW

WINNING WITH PEOPLE

DAVID SIMPSON

Bethany Baptist Church
2353 E. GRAND BLANC ROAD
GRAND BLANC, MICH. 48439
PHONE 694-895

VISION™
HOUSE
PUBLISHING, INC.
Gresham, Oregon 97030

IT'S WHO YOU KNOW: WINNING WITH PEOPLE

© 1995 by David Simpson

Published by Vision House Publishing, Inc.
1217 NE Burnside, Suite 403
Gresham, Oregon 97030

Edited by Val Bechtold
and Chip McGregor

Printed in the United States of America

International Standard Book Number: 1-885305-21-4

All rights reserved. No part of this publication may be reproduced,
stored in a retrieval system, or transmitted, in any form or by any means,
electronic, mechanical, photocopying, recording, or otherwise,
without prior written permission. For information contact:
Vision House Publishing, Inc.

Unless otherwise indicated, all Scripture references are from the
New American Standard Bible, The Lockman Foundation
© 1960, 1962, 1963, 1968, 1971, 1972, 1973, 1975, 1977.
Used by permission.

Thank You, words and music by Ray Boltz.
© 1988 Gaither Music Company ASCAP. Used by permission.

95 96 97 98 99 00 01 02 03 04 — 10 9 8 7 6 5 4 3 2 1

To:

My Father
and
Linda, my wife.

To my father, for instilling within me "the dream"
and to my wife for being a partner in making "the dream" a reality.
You have both impacted me more than I will ever know
or could ever hope to repay.

CONTENTS

ACKNOWLEDGMENTS

On the wall of my office is a picture of a rowing team gliding across the surface of a calm body of water, all members seemingly synchronized in their movement. The caption reads:

Teamwork is the ability to work together toward a common vision. The ability to direct individual accomplishment toward organizational objectives. It is the fuel that allows common people to obtain uncommon objectives.

This quote encapsulates both the essence of this book and the process by which this book came into being.

The Team included many people:

Val Bechtold was not only my editor but also coach and cheerleader.

Marilyn Smith spent many hours in front of a computer monitor while trying to decipher my handwriting. Two librarians, *Corinne Ronald* and *Carla Hoffman* worked diligently to obtain resources that were invaluable to this project.

Ian Lawson and *Dr. Paul Magnus* granted permission to pursue this project in the midst of my teaching load.

I would also like to thank *John Van Diest* and his team at Vision House who believed in this project and worked hard to make it happen.

My six-year-old son, Scott, has been learning some new words lately. After a few hours of playing with the neighborhood kids, Scott comes home and shares some of his new discoveries. The new words stand out because they aren't part of our normal household conversation! My wife and I usually ask Scott where he learned these new words, and he gives one of his playmates proper credit. Scott rarely knows the meaning of the word or phrase, but as he associates with these youngsters, their vocabulary slowly merges to become his vocabulary.

And so it is with adults.

We become like the people we spend time with.

The shape of your relationships determines, in large measure, the shape of your life: "You make your friends, then your friends make you." The German poet Goethe observed, "The greatest genius will not be worth much if he pretends to draw exclusively from his own resources."

Relationships are one of the primary vehicles for communicating values. When a relationship has a negative influence on a person's life we may refer to it as "peer pressure." Conversely, when a relationship has a positive influence on a person's life, we call it "relational empowerment."

We need to align ourselves with people who enhance our ability to grow. And we cannot underestimate the need to intentionally cultivate a network of meaningful and supportive relationships.

When heads of government take office, one of their first duties is to select people for a cabinet. They recognize that without a support group they will never be able to realize their vision. Surrounding yourself with the right people is as critical for you as it is for any political leader. Having positive, mutually edifying relationships is vital to your advancement in work and in your personal development.

Casey Stengel, former manager of the New York Yankees, understood the power of association in shaping a ball player's success. Billy

Martin remembers Stengel's advice to him when Martin was a rookie manager: "There will be fifteen players on your team who will run through the wall for you, five who hate you and five who are undecided. When you make out your rooming list, always room your losers together. Never room a good guy with a loser. Those losers who stay together will blame the manager for everything, but it won't spread if you keep them isolated."

As adults, we like to think that we have matured enough to be unaffected by the values and perspectives of our peers and associates. This belief has no basis in fact, however, for adults are not immune to peer pressure. I know a police officer who was a very positive, upbeat person. He liked his job and believed he was doing something important. Unfortunately, he rode with the same partner in the same cruiser eight hours a day for two years, and his partner had a negative, cynical attitude about everything and everybody. After a while, my friend's enthusiasm began to wane. He began to dread work as a result of constant exposure to his partner. He stopped seeing his role as important and began to believe he was just another cog in the wheel of society.

Association is a two-edged sword; our alliances can stimulate and empower us or they can discourage and weaken us.

While it is important for us, as Christians, to always remember our responsibility to uplift others who may need encouragement, I believe that God also wants us to bring associates into our lives who will empower us and enhance our effectiveness—so that we will be "all that we can be."

The concept of deliberately bringing people into your life who can help you achieve your fullest potential is called "relational empowerment."

Relational empowerment is the enhancing and sharpening of one individual via another. Proverbs recognizes the potential of this force when it states, "As iron sharpens iron, so one individual sharpens another" (Proverbs 27:17).

Highly effective people realize that other people contribute much to their personal success. According to Dr. John Maxwell, author of *Developing the Leader Within You* and pastor of a 3,500-member San Diego church, the most important leadership principle you can discover is "those closest to the leader will determine the level of success for that leader."[1]

Maxwell's assertion is based on the assumption that you are already operating at your optimum level of effectiveness; that you have achieved all you can on your own. If you intend to move beyond this state in your development, you will have to extend your capabilities and influence through certain people in your constellation of relationships: boss, spouse, family, peers, friends, secretary and subordinates. And because these people will play key roles in determining the level of your personal and professional effectiveness, it is imperative that you consistently nurture these relationships, once you develop them.

I've written this book to help you understand why some people are more successful, both professionally and personally, than others. And I want you to understand precisely how others can help you achieve your career and personal goals. I want you also to know how to recruit a team of people who will support you, help you, and advise you—a team to whom you can turn for wisdom and guidance.

According to a recent study, great achievers can usually identify three to ten people who have made significant contributions to their development and ongoing effectiveness.[2] Perhaps, via these pages, I can expedite your finding and cultivating those people—because I want you to be the *greatest* of great achievers.

Notes

[1] John Maxwell, *Developing the Leader Within You* (Nashville, Tenn.: Thomas Nelson Publishers, 1992), 158.

[2] Paul Stanley and Robert Clinton, *Connecting: The Mentoring Relationships You Need to Succeed in Life* (Colorado Springs, Colo.: NavPress, 1992), 11.

CHAPTER ONE

RELATIONSHIPS THAT MAKE A DIFFERENCE

You are the same today
As you will be five years from now
Except for two things—
The books you read and the poeple you meet..
CHARLIE 'T' JONES

Everyone needs a network of meaningful relationships.

Everyone is shaped by those relationships.

And the best of those relationships don't just happen.

Willard Reeves, the great running back of the Canadian Football League's Winnipeg Blue Bombers, often won player-of-the-game honors during his career. One year he won five television sets! Each time Reeves won he gave the prize to one of his offensive linemen—whose performance had boosted his own success. His expression of gratitude follows the leadership principle that *those closest to the leader will determine the level of success of that leader.*

You are empowered by those around you, so—if you want to succeed beyond your own abilities—it is imperative that you develop your relational network.

Perhaps the best place to begin understanding relational networking and the social dynamic of connecting is by understanding what relational networking is *not*. There are four major misconceptions about our personal associations.

1. I don't need anyone else's assistance.

Our society exalts self-sufficiency as the highest virtue. We are emerging from the '70s and '80s, during which the dominant values in our society were individualism and selfishness. The majority of self-help books focused on developing self-image, identifying goals, improving attitude, enhancing work productivity and focusing on personal desires.[1] Susan Hayward, who conducts the *Yankelovich Monitor,* a study of American values, reports that the nineties will see "a social revolution as big as the one that took place in the sixties. We've given up our focus on the rights of self, and we've decided that connection with other people is a tremendously important part of what we want out of life."[2]

We have all heard the testimonies of people who "pulled themselves up by their bootstraps." These successful individuals claim they conquered the odds through bull-headed determination. The reality is that there are few self-made individuals; everyone needs help along the way. Even Lee Iacocca, who epitomized the 1980s version of corporate success, could never have pulled off the greatest corporate transformation in the history of the United States without the help of others. It was former Ford employees who came over to Chrysler and helped craft the K car and Magic Wagon designs—both of which were instrumental in making the turnaround.

Christians have their own version of the myth of self-sufficiency: 'I don't need anyone but Christ in my life." Although this absolute truth describes the source of our salvation, it does not provide a biblical basis for our day-to-day life. God created man for relationships. Scripture clearly teaches that we are to be interdependent. Solomon, considered by many to be the wisest man who ever lived, noted, "Two are better than one, because they have good return for their work: if one falls down a friend can help him up. But pity the man who falls and has no one to help him up!" (Ecclesiastes 4:9–12).

You need the help of others.

2. Networking is a form of manipulation.

Networking often gets associated with con artists—people who try to get close to others, not because they care about them or even like them, but for the sole purpose of manipulating them to further their personal aspirations. Such people think nothing of phoning strangers and passing out business cards at every social function they attend, and we rightly regard them as "networking barracudas."

Many such high achievers are indeed ruthless, believing that "If I'm going to win, you must therefore lose." As one human resource executive put it, "There are people out there who believe that the world is a finite pie, and they can only get ahead by taking away others' shares from them." But the win/lose scenario is seriously out-of-date, whether on a personal or corporate level. Many productive people today are advocating a "win-win or no deal" approach to people management. But successful people have learned the habit of taking into consideration the needs of their co-workers. Rather than establishing contacts for the purpose of personal advancement, *biblical* networking involves developing genuine, permanent, mutually supportive relationships, both personal and professional.

3. High-achievers succeed through talent and technical skill.

J. Paul Getty, when asked what was the most important quality for a successful executive, replied, "It doesn't make much difference how much other knowledge or experience an executive possesses; if he is unable to achieve results through people, he is worthless as an executive." John D. Rockefeller also believed that personal effectiveness is much less dependent on hard work and knowledge than on the ability to work with people: "I will pay more for [it] than for any other ability under the sun."

According to sociologist Michael Zey, talent and technical skills—although necessary for success—are "at best prerequisites."[3] Both the Carnegie Institute of Technology and the Stanford Research Institute agree that in any business endeavor 15 percent of the financial success one achieves is determined by technical knowledge and the other 85 percent is determined by the ability to work with people.

4. Highly effective people eventually outgrow their need for support.

Nothing is further from the truth. Highly effective people know that those in their constellation of relationships will always play a vital role in their success. Rather than abusing those relationships through neglect, disrespect, or selfishness, they have learned to value them, to cultivate them, and to think "effectiveness with people, efficiency with things."

What Is a Relational Network?

Now that we have looked at what networking is not, let's examine what it is.

Networking is the way most things happen.

Even though it is a relatively new term, it is an old idea, once generally associated with the business community. Great achievers have always understood the necessity of "organized assistance."[5] According to John Naisbett, author of the bestseller *Megatrends,* "Networks are people talking to each other, sharing ideas, information, and resources."[6]

A relational network is essentially a cluster of relationships with people you know and have contact with. For some this network is small and limited; for others it is large and expansive.

Identifying Your Existing Network

Our relationships have the potential to influence us either positively, through relational empowerment, or negatively, through peer pressure or "toxic relationships." What counts is not the quantity of people in our constellation, but rather the quality of the relationships we have cultivated. The Relational Constellation pictured below illustrates the kinds of relationships we need to develop:

Your Relational Network

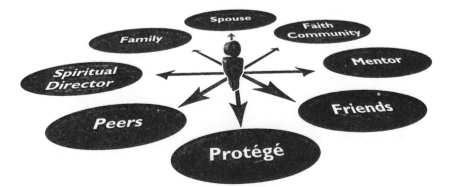

Some of these relationships may already be functioning in your present constellation. Others may need to be established. The number of people that perform these roles may vary and may change over the course of your life.

Building Your Relational Network

The first step in developing a relational network is to take out your daily calendar and evaluate your use of time. Who are the people you have spent more than ten minutes with over the course of the last three weeks? Are they the people you want to be spending your time with? What counts is not whether we have a network (everybody does) but rather what kind of network we have.

We can take either a proactive or reactive approach to building a network. Most associations just happen. Friends become friends because of a common interest: sports, crafts, children, gardening—anything that you share in common. Most people establish the significant relationships in their lives on the basis of such random selection.

If you have taken such a reactive approach to the selection of your associates, you will likely feel "surrounded by people who have taken control of your life. They call you and dictate where you'll be tonight, what you'll do this weekend, what projects you will do next, and how you will spend your casual hours. They have decided to influence, perhaps even direct, your life."[6] If the people who occupy your life are people you did not choose to fill that role, your life is out of control. You are *reactive*, living under the direction of others.

Our lives will invariably be filled with interchanges with people. The question is not, "Will your calendar be full?" but rather, "Who will fill your calendar?" The proactive approach to networking involves selecting the people with whom you are going to spend time. In the words of businessman and author Fred Smith, "Successful networking isn't an accident. It just doesn't happen. For some, using the network is intuitive, but most of us have to learn to use our network constructively."[7]

Is it wrong for Christians to develop intentional relationships?

Consider Jesus' healing encounter with a demon-possessed man in Mark 5:1–20. After being miraculously healed, the man indicates his desire to follow Jesus everywhere. Mark's biography records "…the man who had been demon-possessed begged to go with him. Jesus did not let him…" (vs. 18).

Was the man's request unreasonable? No. Jesus recognized the necessity of being intentional in the selection of his relational constellation. Jesus knew that if he was ever going to accomplish his mission, he needed to spend time training a handful of men. So one night Jesus went off by himself to a mountain and spent the entire night in prayer. The next morning, he called all his followers together and chose twelve to be his disciples. For the remaining years of his ministry—while he didn't ignore the multitudes—he concentrated on those twelve men.

The point is clear: Jesus, after careful thought and prayer, chose the people he wanted around him. They didn't choose him. And even among his disciples he had a much smaller circle of intimates: Peter, James, and John. *Highly effective people have learned that those in their constellation play an indispensable function in their own growth and effectiveness.* Rather than abuse these relationships through neglect, disrespect, or selfishness, they have learned the value of nurturing them.

Action Steps

It takes more than motivation to cultivate valuable relationships; you will need a procedure to follow.

1. *List all the people* who make up your present network of relationships—the people with whom you interact on a regular basis.

2. *Ask yourself two questions* about each of your associations:

   • What kind of person am I becoming as a result of this relationship?

   • What kind of Christian am I becoming as a result of this relationship?

You may discover that some of your friends exert a negative influence on you, and that you therefore need to prayerfully consider decreasing time spent associating with them. Or in some cases you may need to break the tie completely.

There are negative, small-souled, narrow-minded Christians who will not necessarily have a positive influence on your life. You may consider limiting the influence such people have in your life. Choose rather to spend time with those who inspire you, stimulate your thinking, restore your vision and strengthen your competency.

Notes

¹ Michael Zey, *Winning With People: Building Lifelong Professional and Personal Success Through the Supporting Cast Principle* (Los Angeles: J.P.Tarcher, 1990), 5–8

² Susan Hayward quoted in Philip Earnest Johnson, *Time Out! Restoring Your Passion for Life, Love and Work* (Toronto: Stoddart Publishing Co., 1992), 62.

³ Zey, op. cit., 56

⁴ John Naisbitt, *Megatrends: Ten New Directions Transforming Our Lives* (New York: Warner Books, 1982), 192.

⁵ Fred Smith, *You and Your Network* (Waco, Tex.: Word Publishers, 1984), 35.

⁶ Bob Shank, *Total Life Management* (Portland, Oreg.: Multnomah Press, 1990), 14.

⁷ Fred Smith, op. cit., 36.

CHAPTER TWO

YOUR FRIENDS

"The better part of one's life consists of one's friendships."
ABRAHAM LINCOLN

Friendships are one of our most fulfilling sources of happiness.

Research shows that friends can have a very positive influence on our enjoyment of life, personal growth, and personal change. University of Chicago psychologist Mihaly Csikszentmihalyi, (studying the psychology of optimal human experience) indicates that more than anything else "the quality of life depends on two factors: how we experience work, and *our relationships with other people.*" [1]

Obviously, as Christians we believe that an intimate and life-transforming relationship with Jesus Christ is another factor in the happiness equation. But in our daily human existence, our friendships also play a significant role in the enjoyment of life.

It's God's plan for us to be social creatures who need and enjoy others —He has made us people who need people. When the Creation was nearly finished, God observed the relational isolation of His ultimate creation, Adam, and said, "It is not good for the man to be alone" (Gen. 2: 18). As a result He created companionship.

Everyone has this inherent need for relational intimacy. We all have a deep-seated desire to love and be loved, to be accepted by others, and to feel a sense of belonging. Author and pastor Gordon MacDonald says, "As human beings created in the image of God we are essentially relational. That is our most unique quality. Relationships among human beings provide far more than just a basis for mutual survival. Relationships enable us to grow toward the potential of our God-designed humanity. We grow because we encourage each other, because we affirm one another, because we rebuke one another, we support and defend one another."[2]

As relational beings we desire intimacy on two levels. On one level we crave spiritual intimacy, a sense of oneness between ourselves and our Creator. That is a vertical relationship. On another plane we are also desirous of intimacy on a human level. That is a horizontal relationship.

Sometimes people try to have one level compensate for the absence of the other. For example, some married couples express disappointment that their spouses do not meet all their needs. They feel a restlessness in their soul and interpret that inner turmoil as dissatisfaction in their marriage. Somehow marriage is not bringing the deep-seated satisfaction that they expected going into it. As a result they look for some other relationship, whether it be an adulterous one or a new marriage partner, to quench this inner restlessness. Unfortunately in time the inner turmoil resurfaces again. These people are attempting to substitute human intimacy for spiritual intimacy—and it does not satisfy.

Conversely, some people try to have their spiritual intimacy be a substitute for their lack of human relationships. Dietrich Bonhoeffer said, "Nothing can make up for the absence of someone we love, and it would be wrong to try to find a substitute. It is nonsense to say that God fills the gap; He does not fill it, but on the contrary, He keeps it empty and so helps us to keep alive our former communion with each other, even at the cost of pain."

The book of Proverbs has a lot to say about relationships on the horizontal level, and friendships in particular. Solomon, writer of many of the Proverbs, observed some 4,000 years ago; "Perfume and incense bring joy to the heart, and the pleasantness of one's friend springs from his earnest counsel" (Prov. 27:9). He also noted that there are differences in the quality of friendships: "A man of many friends comes to ruin, but there is a friend who sticks closer than a brother" (Prov. 18:24).

Friendships impact our lives in many profound ways. One is that our friendships bring about personal change within us. John Powell says:

> There is a persistent, if uninformed suspicion in most of us that we can solve our own problems and be the masters of our own ships of life, but the fact of the matter is that by ourselves we can be consumed by our problems and suffer shipwreck. What I am, at any given moment in the process of my becoming a person, will be determined by my relationships with those who love me or refuse to love me, with those whom I love or refuse to love. [3]

It is the people in our lives who bring us the most happiness. As someone once said, "when the chemistry of two or more people harmonizes, a dynamic relationship emerges that is difficult to quench."

Men without Friends

Too many men past the age of thirty don't have friends. I have discovered in the course of private conversations that most men have very few close relationships. They have many acquaintances, people with whom they can share a cup of coffee or discuss the results of last night's hockey game, but extremely few—if any—relationships with whom they can discuss the things that matter most.

Many have speculated why this is so. Time pressures are one factor. During their thirties and forties men focus on career and family to the exclusion of friendship. "The demands of making a living, creating and maintaining a home, fulfilling church and job responsibilities and other time pressures make deep relationships a luxury."[4] Most men feel privileged if they can hold a family together, let alone a circle of friends.

But time struggles are not the only obstacle men have to overcome. Sam Keen, in his best selling book about men, *Fire in the Belly,* says that friendship among men "is an endangered species. Friendship doesn't thrive in a social ecology that stresses speed, constant preoccupation, and competition between men...American men are homophobic, afraid of close friendships with other men. The moment we begin to feel warmly toward another man, the 'homosexual' panic button gets pushed."[5]

In addition to these factors, we live in a society that exalts self-sufficiency. We like to be do-it-yourself people. We don't like to have other people dependent on us and we certainly don't want to think we need anyone else. We think we are more than capable to deal with all the complexities of life by ourselves.

According to author Larry Letich the primary factor for the shortage of friendship among men is "that our culture discourages it." Letich adds that within our middle-class framework, "maintaining one's lawn is more important than maintaining one's friendships."[6] As a result, it is not uncommon for men, particularly men in the mid-course of their lives, to discover that they are very lonely. If you were to ask them who their close friends are, most would say, "I don't have any close friends."

As a result of our relational isolation men have become lonely individuals. The American novelist Thomas Wolfe observed, "The whole conviction of my life now rests upon the belief that loneliness, far from being a rare and curious phenomenon, peculiar to myself and a few other solitary men, is the central and inevitable fact of human existence."[7]

Why have men lost their ability to make close friendships? Why do men look back on their high school and college days as the last time they had close friends? Many have suggested that men have probably spent so much of their energies establishing *functional* success that they have not taken the time to think about *relational* success. Men tend to be more task-oriented, while women are inclined to be more relationally oriented.

"Executives and manager males in particular tend to take a particular approach to living that we can describe as striving for mastery and an avoidance of intimacy. Striving for mastery is characterized by emphasis on task accomplishment; by perception of other people as work roles, human assets, or instruments for getting the work done; and by reliance on rational analysis in making decisions. Avoidance of intimacy is characterized by a relative lack of empathy and compassion, inattention to our own and others' feelings, reluctance to experience and express vulnerability and self-doubt, and discomfort in being playful and spontaneous."[8]

In a ten-year study of adult relationships researcher Michael McGill concluded: "To say that men have not intimate friends seems on the surface too harsh...But the data indicates that it is not far from the truth. Even the most intimate of friendships (of which there are few) rarely approach the depth of disclosure a woman commonly has with many other women...Men do not value friendship."[9]

Many men say that their wives are their best friends. They say, "I don't need any other friends—my wife is my best friend." Psychologist and author David G. Meyers in his study of happiness says that men tend to view their wives as their best friend.[10] However, notes Meyers, wives do not often feel the same way about their husbands.

While it might sound impressive to have your wife as your best and only friend, it is very shallow. This puts a great deal of pressure on the marriage. There is no way any one person can meet all the emotional needs of another person. As one person wisely put it, "Your mate should be your best friend, but not your only friend."

Types of Relationships

There are four types of friendships that men rarely move beyond.[11] One is the *friendship of convenience*. In these relationships the basis of the relationship is the exchange of favors. Over the years I have had several of these. For instance, I help Bob move a freezer and he lends me his garden shears.

The second type are *friendships that evolve from doing things together*. These are friendships in which you share mutual interests: football, computers, hunting, et cetera. You simply enjoy doing things together. As Eugene Kennedy of Loyola University puts it, "There is nothing wrong with doing things together, but it isn't true friendship."[12]

The third kind is the *"part-of-a-couple" friendship*. I married at twenty-nine. Up to that time much of my relational energies were spent with other guys my age, usually single. When I did marry, many of those single friends were replaced with other couples.

Most married men rely on their wives to arrange and control the social calendar. As a result men will spend time with other men primary because the wives get along so well. The relationships are not initiated by either of the males, so they might not share anything in common—or even enjoy each other's company.

Last, there are *milestone friendships*. These are friends with whom we share meaningful experiences from our past, but whose friendships are not necessarily now growing and vibrant. For several years a group of my friends from college gathered for an annual Christmas party. Each year new members were included—special friends or spouses. Despite the inclusion of new people, the topic of conversation remained rather consistent. The same stories were retold in all their glory complete with eyewitness accounts and sound effects. Rather than moving forward, this group celebrated a milestone of the past. It was always nice to get together, but the friendships were not growing.

How do they grow?

The Dynamics of Relationships

Author Peter Stein in his report on men and their friends concludes that a sense of "reciprocity appeared crucial in sustaining friendships."[13] Essential ingredients are *acceptance, openness* and *commitment*. All three develop in a reciprocal fashion.

• Reciprocal Acceptance

When we communicate acceptance to another person it involves accepting that person for who he or she is—not what we want that person to become. Carl Rogers says, "True friendship cannot be built until we destroy the idea of what the other person should be."[14] Acceptance is foundational to building a lasting friendship.

My High school friend Tim Clayton has been that kind of friend to me. He has seen me at my best; he has seen me at my worst. We both have enough "ammunition" to do serious harm to each other's reputation. But what has solidified that friendship since our high school days has been the willingness to accept each other. Despite the failures, disappointments and hurt feelings, I have always felt that I never had to pretend to be something other than what I was for Tim. There was never any danger of rejection. I expect and hope that it was that way for him as well.

Dinah Maria Mulcokcraig describes the acceptance that is part of true friendship this way:

> Oh, the comfort, the inexpressible comfort of feeling safe with a person; having neither to weigh the thoughts nor measure the words, but pour them all out, just as they are, chaff and grain together, knowing that a faithful hand will take and sift them, keeping what is worth keeping, and then, with a breath of kindness, blow the rest away. [15]

• *Reciprocal Disclosure*

Most men acknowledge having other men in their network of relationships with whom they enjoy playing golf or talking politics. They enjoy a degree of companionship with colleagues and work buddies. As long as the conversation doesn't get too personal, they feel at ease.

According to British sociologist Marion Crawford, middle-age men and women define friendship differently. "By an overwhelming margin, women talked about trust and confidentiality, while men described a friend as 'someone to go out with' or 'someone whose company I enjoy.' For the most part, men's friendships revolve around activities while women's revolve around sharing."[16] There is value in 'doing things together' but *real* friendship must be established and maintained by sharing information and feelings.

There are five levels of communication that people can experience. The five levels are presented in inverse order, with five being the lowest level of meaningful communication and one being the highest. By understanding these levels you can begin to evaluate the quality of your relationships.

The fifth level is the *cliché conversation* level. It is the kind of conversation that occurs generally around the photocopier at the office, at the mall while you are out shopping, or passing someone on the street. Conversation usually follows predictable patterns, "How are you?"; "I'm fine; how are you?"; "Oh, I'm doing OK" People often refer to this level of communication as small talk. It is safe and you are not obligated to reveal much about yourself. In our hectic schedules it allows us to be maintain social contact without much involvement. Sometimes we simply don't have the time to engage in more meaningful conversation.

Level four is *reporting facts*. Conversation at this level revolves around the disclosure of events. People may talk about what they did on the weekend, what their kids are doing, or what plans they have for summer vacation.

Level three includes our *personal ideas and judgments*. At this level the conversation shifts slightly from discussing things that are external to us to revealing things about ourselves. We may disclose our opinion about something that is going on at the office, at church or about government policy.

Level two is our *feelings and emotions*. This is a deeper level than expressing our opinions on something. It involves revealing our emotional experiences. "I'm disappointed with how my son is doing in school." "I feel angry at the way she treats me." In level two communication you reveal how things make you feel.

Level one is *complete emotional and personal communication*. This is when you can communicate your true self. It is also referred to as "peak communication"—those times in a relationship when people feel free to express absolute openness and honesty.

Looking over these five levels, it is obvious that we can't relate at level one all the time or with everyone. There are people that we only relate to at levels four and five. But it is imperative that we have individuals within our circle of friends with whom we enjoy greater levels of intimacy. Every man needs an intimate friend with whom he can share his true self; not simply talk about his job and his family.

What people discover is that during the natural course of friendship, they become closer as they know more and more about each other. Most relationships start slowly. People disclose the things they like and dislike, their opinions and preferences. One such friend of mine was Rob—my rival in tennis. Our friendship was not limited to the courts, however; we spent late nights talking about our jobs, relationships with women, the impact of our religious heritage on our respective lives, and aspirations we had for our futures.

Sadly, there may be people that you have known for years, but with whom conversation has never developed beyond cliches and the reporting of facts. But self-disclosure is a two-way street. It not only involves one's openness to remove the masks of inauthenticity, it requires listening to others as they disclose at whatever level they feel comfortable revealing.

David Smith, author of *The Friendless American Male* and *Men Without Friends*, tells the story about Queen Victoria's impressions of her two most famous prime ministers. When she was with William Gladstone, she said "I feel I am with one of the most important leaders of the world." Disraeli, on the other hand, "makes me feel as if I am one of the most important people in the world." Reciprocal disclosure requires listening as well as trust. I know of no single step that is as important to building a network of authentic, loving relationships as that of reciprocal self disclosure.

• *Reciprocal Commitment*

There is a prevalent assumption that friendship happens naturally. During adolescence and young adulthood, when so many interests are shared with others and one has great stretches of free time, making friends might seem like a spontaneous process. I have found that having friendships in my adult years requires more intentionality on my part.

When I was pastoring I encouraged some of the other pastors in our area to get together for breakfast once a month. There was no preset agenda, but simply an opportunity for a group of men representing a wide range of age and experience to visit. Certainly there were mornings that the conversation was less than enthralling, but the commitment to be a part of a cadre who met together for mutual encouragement was something I knew I needed to make.

A marvelous example of commitment in friendship is found in the relationship between David and Jonathan. "And Jonathan made a covenant with David because he loved him as himself. Jonathan took off the robe he was wearing and gave it to David, along with his tunic, and even his sword, his bow, and his belt" (1 Samuel 18:1). Jonathan's action was a sign of his commitment. This exchange symbolized the depth of friendship between these two men.

A more contemporary example is found in the relationship that existed between football players Gale Sayers and Brian Piccolo. Gale Sayers was perhaps the best running back the Chicago Bears ever had. He was black. Brian Piccolo, another running back, was also a good athlete but not nearly as talented. He was white. Blacks and whites routinely played on the same professional teams, but these two were different. They were roommates on the road—a first for race relations in football.

Gale Sayers had never before had a close relationship with any white man, and Brian Piccolo admitted that he had never known a black person—not really. But in the span of two brief years, 1967–69, their friendship deepened into one of the most memorable friendships in the history of sports. As the movie "Brian's Song" graphically portrayed, these two men truly loved each other. Part of the reason they grew so close was the tragic fact that Brian Piccolo contracted cancer during the 1969 season. Although he fought to play the season out, he was in the hospital more than he was on the field. As the disease refused to go away, Sayers frequently flew in to be at the bedside of his friend. In time, the smell of death became increasingly more obvious, although the two of them, winners through and through, refused to surrender.

On one occasion both Piccolo and Sayers and their wives were invited to attend the Professional Football Writer's Banquet in New York, where Gale Sayers was to receive the George S. Halas award as "the most courageous player in professional football." By the time of the banquet, Brian Piccolo was too sick to attend. He was confined to his bed at home. As Gale Sayers stood to his feet to receive the award, amid the responding applause of the audience, tears began to flow that he could not restrain. Then he said these words: "You flatter me by giving me this award, but I tell you here and now that I accept it for Brian Piccolo. Brian Piccolo is the man of courage who should receive the George S. Halas award. I love Brian Piccolo and I'd like you to love him, too. Tonight, when you hit your knees, please ask God to love him, too."

How often do we hear adult men say, "I love you" to another man? It is a remarkable and rare statement. Sayers and Piccolo had cultivated more than a superficial tough-guy relationship. Although they were rugged, heterosexual, competitive men to the core, an authentic love had developed between these strong athletes.[17]

Commitment, like acceptance and disclosure, do not occur instantaneously but are cultivated over a long period of time. Commitment is the glue that keeps the relationship together. Our society has a disposable mentality regarding relationships—they are only valuable as long as they are useful. Once they have outlived their usefulness they are quickly discarded. Authentic friendships do not thrive in that kind of environment.

Involvement plus willingness plus time equals commitment.

Barbra Streisand became famous for singing, "People who need people are the luckiest people in the world." Making friends and enjoying friendships are not indicators of one's luck, but indicative of sufficient effort. Intimate friends can be significant contributors to your happiness, your fulfillment, and your success.

Action Steps

How does one go about building a circle of supportive friendships?

1. *Give priority to close friendships.* As long as making friends remains low on your priority list, you'll never find the appropriate time to reach out and touch someone. There are just too many other demands on your time and attention.

   People make all kinds of excuses—they are too busy, they have learned to live without needing anyone, they can't trust people, or they are loners and prefer solitude. But excuses are simply a smoke screen, and underneath lies a powerful aching to love and be loved.

   As long as making friends remains low on your priority list, you'll never find the appropriate time to make friends and establish friendships. There are just too many other matters that demand your attention.

   Few of the valuable things in life "just happen." When they happen it is because we recognize their importance and devote ourselves to them. You can have almost anything you want if you want it badly enough. It is simply a matter of priorities. Significant relationships come to those who assign enough importance to cultivate them.

   Make friendship a high priority.

2. *Be a friend.* This suggestion may seem too obvious to mention, but when you observe the number of unfriendly people in the world who want to love and be loved, the obvious remains a mystery to them. Take the time to listen, to help, and to encourage someone around you. As you intentionally strive to be a friend, you will begin to see friendships develop.

3. *Be selective.* The majority of us know only the people whom we have happened to meet on our way through life. We didn't try to remember them; they just kept running into us along the way and it was easier to archive their names for next time than it was to keep asking who they were. Social contact grew out of this consistent interaction. Friends became friends because of common activity, nothing more. Most of us accept random selection for the most significant relationships of our lives.

The Bible informs believers to select their friends carefully, for your friends can influence you for either good or bad. Recall that Proverbs states, "He who walks with wise men will be wise, but the companion of fools will suffer harm" (13:20). Friends can be a great encouragement to help you develop in your spiritual life if you've chosen friends who also have a personal and growing relationship with God.

Notes

[1] Mihaly Csikszentmihalyi, Flow: *The Psychology of Optimal Experience.* (New York: Harper & Row, 1990), 164 (emphasis added).

[2] Gordon MacDonald, *Living at High Noon.* (Old Tappan, N.J.: Fleming H. Revell), 141–142.

[3] John Powell, *Why Am I Afraid to Tell You Who I Am?.* (Niles, Ill.: Argus Communications, 1969), 43

[4] Edgar Metzler quoted in Ajith Fernando, *Reclaiming Friendship: Relating to Each Other in a Frenzied World.* (Scottsdale, Ariz.: Herald Press, 1993), 13.

[5] Sam Keen, *Fire in the Belly.* (New York: Bantam, 1991), 174.

[6] Larry Letich, "Do you know who your friends are?" *Utne Reader,* May/June 1991: 85–87.

[7] Quoted in Gary Inrig, *Quality Friendships.* (Chicago: Moody Press, 1981), 16.

[8] Joan Kofodimos, *Balancing Act: How Managers Can Integrate Successful Careers and Fulfilling Personal Lives.* (San Francisco: Jossey-Bass, 1993), 6.

[9] Quoted in R. Kent Hughes, *Disciplines of a Godly Man.* (Wheaton, Ill.: Crossway Books, 1991), 60.

[10] David G. Myers, "Pursuing Happiness," *Psychology Today* (July/August 1993): 32–35, 66–67.

[11] Both Paul D. Robbins, "Must Men Be Friendless?" *Leadership,* (Fall 1984), 24–29 and Fred Smith *You and Your Network,* (Waco, Tex.: Word Books, 1984) 140–142 discuss these four types of friendships.

[12] Quoted in Paul Robbins op. cit., 26.

[13] Peter J. Stein, "Men and Their Friendships" in *Men in Families,* ed. Robert A. Lewis and Robert E. Salt. (Beverly Hills: Sage Publications, 1986).

[14] Quoted in Robbins op. cit., 26.

[15] Dinah Maria Mulcokcraig, quoted in Fred Smith op. cit., 167.

[16] Alan Loy McGinnis, *The Friendship Factor.* (Minneapolis: Augsburg Press, 1979), 11.

[17] Quoted in David Wells, *Learning to Love: When Love Isn't Easy.* (Wheaton, Ill.: Victor Books, 1992), 201–202.

CHAPTER THREE

FINDING A MENTOR

Our chief want is someone who will make us
what we know we can become.
EMERSON

If you take an iron poker and stick it in a fire it will collect the heat around it. Eventually it will become red hot. That same principle holds true in the social realm. If we spend our time around people who are "on fire," they in turn may ignite our passion—our passion for life, for people, for family, for work, and for God. Mentors are those people.

Mentoring is a buzzword in business, the arts, and education. It has been described as "the best thing and worst thing that can happen to one's career." Increasingly people are discovering that mentors can help them achieve their professional goals and enhance their personal effectiveness. Bobb Biehl, president of Masterplanning Group International, identifies two primary benefits of having a mentor. First, you get to do most things faster if you have a mentor who will tell you where to go to find a certain resource or show you how to do something. It's a lot easier to learn when you've got a friend who wants you to develop skill and is teaching you on a one-to-one basis. Second, you have available to you the network of the mentor. One of the greatest roles a mentor can play is to introduce a protégé to the right person at the right time.[1]

Much of the material being published on the subject of mentoring deals with the subject almost exclusively from the perspective of career enhancement. The concept of mentoring, however, should be understood much more broadly than this. Let's take a fresh look at this centuries-old tradition.

What is Mentoring?

Contrary to popular opinion, mentoring is not a new idea. The term "mentor" is derived from the name of a character in Homer's *The Odyssey.* In this ancient Greek tale, King Odysseus entrusts his only son, Telemachus, to the care and training of his wise friend, Mentor, while he himself goes off to war. Classical mentoring encompasses the idea of older, more experienced people sharing their knowledge, skills and resources with younger, less experienced people. Indeed, mentoring was the only means of transmitting values, skills, and character qualities from one generation to the next.

"In past centuries, craftsmen of every calling—from carpenters to metal smiths to lawyers to the great painters and composers of the Renaissance—employed young apprentices. These apprentices learned not only the skills and craft of their trades, but such intangible dimensions of their calling as integrity, pride of craftsmanship, honesty, diligence and commitment to excellence."[2]

Mentoring, as understood in contemporary North American culture, is one person having a positive impact on another. John C. Crosby once said, "Mentoring is a brain to pick, a shoulder to cry on, and a kick in the pants." The person sharing his or her resources is called the mentor. The person being empowered is called the mentoree or protégé.

Finding and making use of the right mentor is one of the most critical steps you'll ever take.

There is still the perception in the minds of some that having a mentor is a necessary prerequisite to getting on the fast track to the top. Having a more senior person in the organization who advises you on office politics or who pulls strings to get you a promotion may help escalate your way to success. But mentoring, from a biblical perspective, encompasses a more holistic concept than merely giving oversight to one's career.

"The purpose of mentoring is not merely to impart knowledge to others (although mentoring has an educational dimension). The purpose of mentoring is not merely to impart skills to others (although mentoring has a training dimension as well). Rather, authentic mentoring deals primarily with issues of maturity and integrity, and only secondarily with information and skills. It has much more to do with modeling character than with verbal teaching. It has more to do with what is caught than what is taught."[3]

In the business world mentoring is often defined much more narrowly, usually having a corporate insider overseeing your career. This definition probably brings to mind visions of those who have gained the competence of manipulating the system rather than competence in performing a particular job. But mentoring is much more than overseeing one's career development. It also encompasses the nurturing of one's personal development. I feel more comfortable with the more holistic definition of Stanley and Clinton:

"Mentoring is a relational process between mentor, who knows or has experienced something (resources of wisdom, information, experience, confidence, insight, relationships, status, etc.) to a mentoree, at an appropriate time and manner, so that it facilitates development or empowerment."[4]

The God-given resources may include wisdom, experiences, patterns, habits of obedience, and principles for living and working more successfully. Bobb Biehl has a similar concept in mind when he defines mentoring as "making the mentor's personal strengths, resources and network (friendships/contacts) available to help the protégé reach his or her goals."[5]

Both definitions include the concept of making resources available to assist the protege in reaching his or her goals. Perhaps that is why Gordon MacDonald refers to these people who fill the mentoring void in our lives as "VRPs —Very Resourceful People."[6]

Scripture contains many examples of mentoring, but one of the most outstanding is that of Barnabas, who mentored both Paul and John Mark. He was one of the first to see the potential in Saul (who later became known as Paul), when other Christians were afraid to have anything to do with their former persecutor. "But Barnabas took him (Saul) and brought him to the apostles" (Acts 9:27). Barnabas must have encouraged and taught Saul during those early days and patiently stayed with him, knowing that time and experience would soon temper and mature this gifted young leader.

Sometimes it takes someone else believing in us before we can have the confidence to believe in ourselves. Eric Butterworth, in "Love: the One Creative Force," tells this story: "A college professor had his sociology class go into the Baltimore slums to get case histories of 200 young boys. They were asked to write an evaluation of each boy's future. In every case the students wrote, 'He hasn't got a chance.' Twenty-five years later another sociology professor came across the earlier study. He had his students follow up on the project to see what had happened to those boys. With the exception of 20 boys who had moved away or died, the students learned that 176 of the remaining 180 achieved more than ordinary success as lawyers, doctors and businessmen.

"The professor was astounded and decided to pursue the matter further. Fortunately, all the men were in the area and he was able to ask each one, 'How do you account for your success?' In each case the reply came with feeling: 'There was a teacher.'

"The teacher was still alive, so he sought her out and asked the old but still alert lady what magic formula she had used to pull these boys out of the slums into successful achievement.

"The teacher's eyes sparkled and her lips broke into a gentle smile. 'It's really very simple,' she said. 'I loved those boys.'"[7]

What Are the Benefits of Having a Mentor?

Mentors can play a variety of supportive roles in our lives, among them *advisor, coach,* and *role model.*

Advisor

The Bible portrays God as guiding us. Psalm 73:24 says, "You guide me with your counsel." God at times leads directly in our lives and there are times when He leads through other people.

We live in an age that values self-sufficiency and individualism, that regards other people as valuable only insofar as they "help me get what I want." The self-sufficient person considers it a weakness to ask other people for advice. Unfortunately, these same secular attitudes are also held by many Christians.

I had lunch one day with Mark, a talented young manager of a retail store. He regarded his present job as a fast track to nowhere. He knew he had to make a career move but didn't know in what direction. Since I was unacquainted with Mark's background, I asked him, "Mark, who are the people you turn to for wise counsel?"

"Besides my wife, no one," was his reply.

"Is that because you have no one in the city who knows you well enough to assist you during your decision-making?" I asked.

"That's part of it," he said, "but mostly I never thought about discussing it with anyone."

His response, so typical of his generation, stands in contrast to the wisdom found in the book of Proverbs: "Where there is no guidance the people fall, but in the abundance of counselors there is victory" (Prov. 11:14).

Some business executives serve as advisors by helping their clients to step back and see the big picture, to put things into perspective. A growing number of top executives are finding that they, too, need someone to come into their private world and help sort out motives, strengthen values, and encourage right thinking and action. For many executives this type of personal guide is not a frivolous benefit but a necessity.

We should consider such advisors to be a lifelong necessity instead of seeking them only during our formative years. Sometimes there is a tendency to view advisors or mentors as we view school: important in the formative years of one's life but eventually outgrown. Guidance and wise counsel is something we need all of our lives.

I can specifically recall several conversations I had with one of my mentors. It was during a time of intense personal struggle.

"You know, John," I said, "I think I made a mistake accepting the invitation to join the staff of this church."

"What do you mean?" John asked.

"I don't perceive that my vision for this church is compatible with several of the other staff members. I sense at times we are pursuing different visions for ministry." I further explained that my expectations coming into this position had not materialized, nor was it looking promising in the near future.

In addition to being an active listener, my mentor challenged me to reassess my position. He highlighted the possible implications my decision would have on my career. His perspective provided invaluable assistance at a critical point in my development. I had tunnel vision; he had an aerial view.

Most of us, if we had a medical or a legal problem, would not make a decision without first consulting an advisor, someone with expertise in the relevant field. That same principle ought to hold true in other areas of our lives. Indeed, we need more than one advisor. In our increasingly complex world we ought to aim for a sort of "board of directors"— people of integrity, preferably Christians, who know us well and can give advice in every dimension of life, from career decisions to legal counsel to health tips. We ought to be wise enough to see advisors who will provide not only encouragement, but constructive criticism as well. Moreover, we need to request their help before we encounter crises.

Early in my ministry I was fortunate to have Dr. William McRae as a mentor. One day Dr. McRae, who was the senior pastor of the church where I worked, came into my office and indicated to me that I was beginning to develop some habits that could be very detrimental to the effectiveness of my ministry. He noted that periodically I lacked sensitivity to the women who voluntarily served in our secretarial pool at the church and that periodically my priorities at work were not properly aligned. Since I respected him and knew that he had my best interests in mind I felt compelled to take corrective action on the basis of what he said. The book of Proverbs says, "He who listens to a life-giving rebuke will be at home among the wise" (Prov. 15:31). A mentor can bring that kind of helpful advice to your life.

Coach

A second benefit you can receive from a mentor is to have someone close to you serve as your personal "coach." Whereas a mentor who functions as an advisor counsels us on important decisions, a mentor may also function as a coach, seeking to expand our competency through the development of particular skills. The mentor-as-coach, like the coach of an athletic team, may relationally empower through motivation and training. "An experienced coach does not try to control the player (or mentoree), but rather he seeks to inspire and equip him with the necessary motivation, perspective, and skills to enable him to excellent performance and effectiveness."[8]

In his autobiography, Al Neuharth, founder of the newspaper *USA Today*, told the poignant story about being coached in the nuances of business life. Neuharth moved to Detroit to become assistant to the executive editor of the *Detroit Free Press*. Shortly after his arrival he was invited to lunch by Jack Knight, owner of the Knight-Ridder newspaper chain, of which the *Press* was a part. They went around the corner to the entrance of the posh Detroit Club, when suddenly Jack Knight said, "Let's go."

A surprised Neuharth asked, "Aren't we going to have lunch?"

Knight replied, "Yeah, let's go," and he started walking.

Neuharth was led six blocks to the basement lunch counter in the old Woolworth Five and Dime store. There, Jack Knight ordered a hot dog and coke and asked Neuharth what he wanted. Al had the same. Here was this immaculately dressed multimillionaire, a Pulitzer prize-winning writer in his own right and one of America's most powerful media moguls, handing Al a hot dog with mustard and ketchup.

Knight said, "The editor will give you memberships in the Detroit Club and the Athletic Club, and take you to meet the mayor and a lot of other civic leaders, and after a while you think you are writing for them. But remember, a lot of people who buy our newspapers eat here every day. Ask them what they read."

"And remember," Knight continued after a pause, "don't become a captive of your own comfort. Keep your feet on the street. Don't eat at the Detroit Club every day." Neuharth links that experience directly to the decision made years later to design *USA Today* as a popular national tabloid.[9]

There are times and circumstances in which we can learn vicariously. A coach can enable us to glean from the experience of other people without necessarily repeating those same mistakes. Because young people can now expect to change jobs or careers anywhere from three to seven times during their lifetime, we probably are in most need of coaches in the years following our formal education. During these inevitable times of transition, we will need to learn new skills. We will also need help to face other crises such as becoming parents, coping with young children, communicating with teenagers, caring for aging parents, planning for retirement, and coping with the empty nest syndrome. During such times our coaches can help us clarify performance goals and developmental needs. The coach may also recommend specific behaviors that need to be improved.

Some of my coaches have been professors who have let me pick their brains after class. I not only tried to get them to expand on the topics they treated during lectures, but also attempted to gain practical wisdom from them that would help me face the problems encountered in ministry. This type of exchange has become increasingly valuable to me during my doctoral studies, for as I reflect on my ministry I notice that I have encountered problems that were never dealt with in my seminary classes.

Role Models

"Example," said Edmund Burke," is the only school of mankind, and they will hear of no other." Modeling is a powerful learning tool.

Dr. Dann Spader of SonLife Ministries in Chicago played a mentoring role during my formative years as a youth pastor. Not only did the principles he taught expand my understanding of youth ministry, but he embodied many of the values I aspired to. Dann always impressed me with his focus in ministry. He reminded me of the Apostle Paul's words, "This one thing I do"—not "these thirty things I dabble in." Dann has a tremendous ability to align all his activities with his mission for life and ministry. Whenever I had the opportunity to spend time with him, one-on-one, I came away inspired and revitalized, eager to return to my ministry. Dann motivated me by his example.

And so we need to seek out positive role models, people who provide a healthy pattern. In days long gone, role models were often selected from among one's community, or from characters read about in books. Now many of our contemporary role models come via the television set. Media personalities such as Bill Cosby and Tim Allen are portrayed as modern and relational father figures. Mother figures come in the form of Murphy Brown and Roseanne Barr.

No one is the perfect role model. Identify each of his or her strengths and work on emulating them. If someone is good with interpersonal relationships, learn from him regarding that one area. Perhaps a person's strengths lie in the area of personal discipline, or vision casting, or problem solving. Emulate them. Lord Chesterfield said it well: "We are more than half of what we are by imitation. The great point is to choose good models and to study them carefully."

One Mentor or a Cluster of Mentors?

Rarely will you find one individual who will fill all the mentoring functions (advisor, coach and role model), but if you identify one specific role that a potential mentor can fill, you have a good beginning.

There is a real danger of idolizing our mentors. "One way to make sure that we avoid the excesses and extremes of a single mentor with an aberrant or malignant personality is to make sure that we have many mentors, not just one."[10] The book of Proverbs also highlights the value of multiple advisors: "Plans fail for lack of wisdom, but with many advisors they succeed" (15:22) and "...many advisors make victory sure" (11:14).

The assumption prevalent in the mentoring literature suggests that a mentor guides you for about five years. In reality that rarely happens. Mentor-protégé relationships often last for a twelve–eighteen month period. "As we develop and mature, we often find the need to change models. Just as we outgrow our need for certain books, we outgrow our need for certain models and need to move on to someone whose desirable traits are on a higher level."[11]

How Do You Select a Mentor?

How does one go about looking for a mentor? What are the necessary qualities that a mentor should possess? Bobb Biehl has what he calls the Mentor Checklist.[12] In it he suggests questions you should ask before establishing a mentor-protégé relationship.

1. Will the mentor be objective, lovingly honest, and provide a balanced source of feedback for your questions? We all have areas in our professional and personal lives that need to be improved. Unfortunately we are not always aware of what they are. That was certainly true when Dr. McRae walked into my office and identified those areas of potential concern. We need people who will be honest enough to illuminate areas of weakness.

2. Will the mentor be open and transparent with his own struggles? Most of us gain a certain degree of encouragement when we know that other people struggle in ways that are similar to our

own. When a mentor has the courage to self-disclose to his protégé, it can be a tremendous source of reassurance to know one is
not alone.

3. Will the mentor model his teachings? Look for someone you
admire. Do you share that person's values and philosophy of life?
Do you admire that person's character qualities—courage, faith,
integrity, compassion, wisdom, discernment, strength and love?
Do you want to grow to possess those same qualities?

4. Does the mentor know and believe in you? Is he one of your
cheerleaders, not your chief critic? Select someone who believes
in people—someone who is committed to relationships, who has
a positive outlook. This doesn't mean you don't ever want to be
confronted by your mentor. The whole point of a mentoring
relationship is to challenge you with new ways of thinking and
doing things, so that you can change and grow. But you want to
make sure that whatever difficulties might arise in the relationship, you will have the kind of mentor who seeks to build you
up, not tear you down.

5. Is the mentor successful in your eyes? Fred Smith says, "Our
selection and use of models is largely controlled by our self-
image. We cannot become what we cannot see ourselves becoming. As we see ourselves, so we draw to ourselves those aids which
develop us. Therefore, it is important for us to see in our models
the person we can and truly want to become".[13]

6. Does the mentor want to see younger people succeed in developing their spiritual and leadership potential? Choose a person who
will genuinely rejoice in your growth and achievements, someone
who is interested in you and pulling for you, not someone who
will feel threatened by your progress.[14] An example of the latter is
the jealousy that King Saul manifested toward David. Even
though David was much younger, the crowds chanting "Saul has
killed his thousands, David has killed his ten thousands," began
to bother him to the point that he actually tried to kill David.
Select someone who will rejoice when you rejoice and weep
when you weep.

The Dynamics of Healthy Mentoring Relationships

Mentoring can be a one-shot intervention or a life-long friendship. It can be carried out informally, as part of a friendship, or formally, as part of a highly structured employee training program.[15] The dynamics that make for a healthy mentoring relationship will vary according to the intensity and length of the relationship. For example, a coaching relationship will often be more intense than that with an advisor or role model. Coaching requires getting together consistently to evaluate progress. The relationship will usually be more short lived than the other two.

According to Paul Stanley and Robert Clinton there are three dynamics that are vital to the mentoring relationships: *attraction, responsiveness,* and *accountability.*[16]

Attraction "is the necessary starting point in the mentoring relationship. The mentoree is drawn to the mentor for various reasons: perspective, certain skills, experience, values, perceived wisdom, position, character, knowledge and influence. The mentor is attracted to the mentoree's attitude, potential and opportunity for influence. As attraction increases, trust, confidence, and mentoring subjects develop that will strengthen the mentoring relationship and ensure empowerment." There has to be a certain chemistry for a mentoring relationship to work.

Responsiveness suggests that "the mentoree must be willing and ready to learn from the mentor. Attitude is crucial for the mentoree. A responsive, receiving spirit on the part of the mentoree and the attentiveness on the part of the mentor directly accelerate and enhance the empowerment." One can initiate the contact but must be careful not to force a relationship. The best mentoring relationships develop naturally. And regardless of how they begin, relationships tend to evolve.

The underlining theme in the book of Proverbs is that those in pursuit of truth must have an attitude of receptivity to truth. Solomon tells us, "Wisdom is found in those who take advice" (Prov. 13:10) and, "He who ignores discipline comes to poverty and shame, but whoever heeds correction is honored" (Prov. 13:18).

Roger Von Oech, in his offbeat-titled book, *A Whack on the Side of the Head,* tells the story about an old Zen master named Nan-ln, who lived in nineteenth century Japan. Nan-In invited one of his students over to his house for afternoon tea. They visited for a while, and then the old man said, "May I serve you some tea?"

"Yes, thank you," the student replied as he seated himself on the ground across a low table from the Zen Master.

Nan-In set a cup before the student and began pouring tea. He talked as he poured, fixing his gaze on the eyes of his visitor. The student was so intent on what Nan-In was saying that it was several moments before he glanced down and saw that the teacup was overflowing and Nan In was still pouring.

Finally the student shouted "Stop, you overfilled the cup !"

Nan-In smiled and stopped pouring. "Yes, my friend, the cup is overfull. You are like this cup, so full of your own ideas and opinions. How can I teach you any wisdom until you first empty the cup?"[17]

Responsiveness is critical to the prótegé.

The third important dynamic in the mentoring relationship is accountability. Mutual responsibility for another in the mentoring process ensures progress and closure. Sharing expectations along with periodic review and evaluation will give strength to application and facilitate empowerment. The mentor should take responsibility for initiating and maintaining accountability with the mentoree.

Action Steps

The action steps you take will depend in large measure on the kind of mentoring relationship you want. Mentoring relationships can be formal or informal. You may simply get along well with another more senior person in your organization, or the company for which you work for may assign you to a mentor. The relationship may be spontaneous or planned. You and your mentor may agree to meet together once or twice a month to discuss your personal and professional goals or you may simply agree to get together whenever a need arises.

If you would like to see something more intentional, the following steps should help to establish such an arrangement:

1. *Pray.* I'm not saying this glibly. God is actively involved in our lives and prayer may be a means God uses to direct us.

2. *Make a short list* of four to six individuals whose company you enjoy. Mentoring, like friendship, works best when it is natural.

3. *Approach one or two* of those individuals and outline your expectations to them.

4. *Allow the individual an opportunity to ponder* your proposal. Obviously he is going to be making a commitment of time and energy. Most people don't invest either of these easily.

5. *Place a time limit* on the relationship. A time frame of six–eighteen months is often a good place to start. After that time both parties can reassess the situation.

Notes

[1] Ted W. Engstrom and Norman B. Rohrer, *The Fine Art of Mentoring: Passing on to Others what God has Given You.* (Brentwood, Tenn.: Wolgemuth & Hyatt, Publishers, Inc. 1989), 103.

[2] Ron Lee Davis, *Mentoring: the Strategy of the Master.* (Nashville, Tenn.: Thomas Nelson, 1991), 19.

[3] Ibid, 45.

[4] Paul Stanley and Robert Clinton, *Connecting: the Mentoring Relationships You Need to Succeed in Life.* (Colorado Springs, Colo.: NavPress, 1992), 40.

[5] Bobb Biehl, "Mentoring: Finding one, Becoming one" Tape. Master Planning Group, 1991.

[6] Gordon MacDonald, *Renewing Your Spiritual Passion.* (Nashville, Tenn.: Oliver Nelson, 1989)

[7] Eric Butterworth, "Love: the one creative force", in *Chicken Soup for the Soul: One Hundred and One Stories to Open the Heart and Rekindle the Spirit,* ed. Jack Canfield and Mark Maasen, (Deerfield, Fla: Heath Communications, 1993), 3–4.

[8] Stanley and Clinton, op. cit., 76.

[9] Gordon F. Shea, *Mentoring: A Practical Guide.* (Menlo Park, Calif.: Crisp Publications Inc. 1992), 11.

[10] Davis, op. cit., 178.

[11] Fred Smith, *You and Your Network.* (Waco, Tex., Word Books, 1984), 89.

[12] Bobb Biehl, op. cit.

[13] Smith, op. cit., 91.

[14] Davis, op. cit., 28–29.

[15] Shea, op. cit., 9.

[16] Stanley and Clinton, op. cit., 10.

[17] Roger Van Oech, *A Whack on the Side of the Head.* (New York: Warren Books, 1983), 10.

CHAPTER FOUR

BEING A MENTOR

If you are planting for a year, plant grain.
If you are planting for a decade, plant trees.
If you are planting for a century, plant people.
ANCIENT WISDOM

There is a legend of a man who was lost in the desert. He stumbled on, dying of thirst, until he came to an abandoned house. Outside the dilapidated, windowless, weather-beaten, deserted shack was a pump. He lurched forward and began pumping furiously, but no water came from the well. Then he noticed a small jug with a cork at the top and a note written on the side: "You have to prime the pump with water, my friend. P. S.—And fill the jug again before you leave." He pulled out the cork and saw that the jug was full of water.

Should he pour it down the pump? What if it didn't work? All of the water would be gone. If he drank the water from the jug, he could be sure he would not die of thirst. But to pour it down the rusty pump on the flimsy instruction written on the outside of the jug?

Something told him to follow the advice and choose the risky decision. He proceeded to pour the whole jug of water down the rusty old pump and furiously pumped up and down. Sure enough, the water gushed out! He had all he needed to drink. He filled the jug again,

BETHANY BAPTIST CHURCH

corked it, and added his own words beneath the instructions on the jug: "Believe me, it really works. You have to give it all away before you can get anything back."[1]

Our society would frown on such a message. We are told to look out for ourselves first and to hoard our resources. But Jesus had a different agenda. In describing the mentoring style of Jesus, Ted Engstrom writes,

> Unlike mentors who are considered successful today, Jesus did not organize His team in order to be served. He never asked them to make him look good. They were never required to wait on Him. Just the opposite was true: He served them. The Master built them up, encouraged them, corrected them, and stretched them as they struggled to receive the truth and obey the will of God. 'Whoever wants to be great among you must be your servant," He taught in Mark 10:43–45, "and whoever wants to be first must be a slave of all. For even the Son of Man did not come to be served, but to serve, and to give his life as a ransom for many." In John 13:15, He said in the upper room after washing their feet, "I have set for you an example that you should do as I have done for you."[2]

The Hunger for Significance

Jesus' life highlighted one of the paradoxes of life: that true significance is found not in self-centered living but in making a difference in the lives of others. Certainly one of the inner cries of people in the '90s is the striving for significance. Of course, some are content to live life in a "survival mode"—pay the bills, make sure the house is in order, and take the minimal amount of risk. Others are not content with merely surviving, they want to be able to "succeed"—to be able to reach their full potential; to be able to enjoy the perks and trappings that come from being successful in the workplace. Yet there are others who are realizing that success and all that accompanies it do not bring the long-lasting, deep-seated fulfillment that they had expected.

Perhaps as a result of the self-centeredness and greed of the '80s, people in the '90s are wanting to experience the feeling that comes from knowing they have done something worthwhile. They want their lives to count. They wish to give their lives to something that will outlast them.

This impacts the way people choose careers: they want positions that will provide fulfillment, a sense of meaning, and a purpose for life. People crave significance. *We want our lives to make a significant difference.*

Mentoring is the process of investing our lives in those who come after us, beginning with our own children, and spreading out to those men and women God brings into our lives. It is wonderful to be assisted by a mentor who helps us navigate through our adult world, but there comes a time in our lives when we have the moral imperative to give back to others and become a part of someone else's supporting cast. As Dietrich Bonhoeffer said, the righteous person is he who lives for the next generation."

Pastor and author Ron Lee Davis identifies the desires of many people when he says, "I feel a need to make a very different kind of investment. I feel an urgency to invest in people, to transmit to another generation the faith and heritage that my mentors have so graciously invested in me."[3]

The process of helping others develop to their full potential is what mentoring is all about. Becoming a people developer involves having the right attitude towards people, providing the necessary resources that will enable people to reach their personal and professional goals, and developing an enriching relationship that will make a significant difference in the life of another.

The Right Attitudes toward People

The attitudes we have toward people will have a profound influence on the way that we treat them. Certainly the most powerful and positive attitude is believing the best about others. Author Alan Loy McGinnis writes:

> More than anything else, it is our attitude towards the people in our classrooms or office that will determine failure or success of motivation. If people know we expect good things from them, they will in most cases go to great lengths to live up to our expectations. If we expect the worst, they will meet those predictions with disappointing accuracy.[4]

Dr. Robert Rosenthal, a Harvard psychologist, conducted several classroom experiments in this area. He took large classes of all ages and randomly divided them into two sections. He would tell teachers that the sharpest students comprised one section and that the other students were just average. After several months of teaching, the section labeled "sharp" achieved on average four points higher on all testing! And the only difference between the two sections was in the mind of the teachers. They believed in the labels. The teachers were amazed when informed of the experiment. They thought that they had not treated either section differently—*but their attitudes towards the students were different.*

My friend Dr. Dann Spader often says, "You cannot not communicate!" People will know your attitude toward them long before you open you mouth. According to psychologist Albert Mehrabian, only 7 percent of our message is communicated through our actual words. The bulk of our message, 93 percent, is communicated through nonverbal cues such as tone of voice, body positioning, and attitudes. If we have a high regard for people it will be communicated; and if we possess a low opinion of others it too will become clear, whether we intend so or not.

Not only is it necessary for leadership to possess a strong belief in people, they must also possess a strong assurance of the work of the Holy Spirit in people's lives. The Church is often guilty of having a pessimistic perspective towards other people: "Oh Joe—he'll never change. He's always been irresponsible." Or "Susan? On this committee? She's not organized. We'd be lucky if she remembers the meetings." Statements such as these reflect a pessimistic view of God's ability to transform people. The apostle Paul envisioned the potential of what God was doing in the lives of the Philippian believers when he wrote, "In all my prayers for you, I always pray with joy...being confident of this, that he who has begun a good work in you will carry it on to completion until the day of Jesus Christ" (Phil. 1:6).

Barnabas was one Christian leader in the Bible who believed that God is in the business of changing people's lives. Do you remember the incident in Acts where the established leaders questioned the authenticity of Paul's conversion experience? Shortly after his radical transformation on the road to Damascus, Paul went to Jerusalem to find the Christian brothers. But the disciples wanted nothing to do with him because they didn't believe that his experience was authentic. Then the narrative records, "But Barnabas took him and brought him to the apostles" (Acts 9:27).

Let's face it, every one of us has flaws and rough edges—we wouldn't be human if we didn't. Unique is the person who can see beyond the exterior and, by focusing on the positive qualities in others, draw the best out of them. Barnabas was that kind of person.

We can choose to build on people's strengths or focus on their weaknesses. Diamond hunters in South Africa have to move several tons of dirt to get a few pebbles, each about the size of your fingernail. They don't seem to mind because they know that what they are looking for is worth the effort. They don't go into the mines looking for dirt; they go in looking for diamonds.

Unfortunately in our human and family relationships there is a natural tendency to focus on the dirt in other people's lives and ignore the diamonds. Sometimes you have to move lots of dirt to find the diamonds in people. Some individuals have the special gift of seeing beyond the dirt in other people's lives and discovering the "diamond-in-the-rough." I have found that if you train your mind to search for the positive things about other people you will be surprised at how many good things you can see in them.

Successful businessman Fred Smith observes, "Some people have a magnetism for iron; no matter who they deal with, they are always attracted to whatever good is in the person. Others have an allergy for clay; they break out in hives over whatever is bad in the people they meet."

The story that follows may be old, but its message is still ahead of its time. It was the custom of the old man to sit outside the wall of the ancient city where he lived, watching passersby come and go. He always sat in the shade, usually surrounded by children, retelling stories which they loved to hear. Through the course of the day, many travelers would stop to chat.

One hot summer day a stranger stopped to visit for a few minutes with the old man, who was entertaining his young friends. The stranger approached the old man and said, 'I'm thinking of moving to your fair city. Tell me, sir, what kind of people live here?"

Quickly the old man replied, "What kind of people live in the city where you're from?"

"The people in my town are unkind" said the stranger. "They cheat and steal and lie. They speak badly of each other. I am leaving that town because of the undesirable people who live there."

The old man gazed sadly at the stranger and said, 'I'm sorry to inform you, but you will find the same type of people in this town."

And without a word the stranger turned and walked away as the old man continued his tale to the children.

A short time later another stranger came down the road toward the gate. He, too, stopped to chat.

He said, "My good man, I need to move to a new town such as yours. Tell me sir, what type of people live here?"

The old man asked this stranger the same question. 'What kind of people live in the town where you're from?"

"The people in my town are good," he replied. "They are friendly, courteous, and are always looking for an opportunity to do a good deed for someone. I truly hated to leave that town because of the warmth and kindness of its people, but my work requires that I move. "

The old man clasped the hand of the traveler and said, "You'll find the same type of people here. Welcome to our fine town." And the stranger walked happily through the gate.

The children sat in silence. Finally, one of them approached the old man and asked, "Why, sir, didn't you tell those men the truth? You told one that our people were bad and the other that they were good."

The old man begged them to sit. "I did tell the truth," he explained. "You see, no matter where you go or what you do, you will find in other people just what you are looking for. *If you search for the good you will find it; but if you look for the bad, that is what you will undoubtedly see.* Almost everyone has far more good qualities than bad. Always look for the best in others." [5]

Having a right attitude involves not only focusing on the best in people, it also involves the willingness to express the best. It is important to make a distinction between appreciation and affirmation. We appreciate what a person does; we affirm him for who he is. There is a significant difference.

Unfortunately, in our culture the focus is often more on appreciation for what a person does for us rather than on affirming people for who they are. In his recent autobiography, hockey star Wayne Gretzky tells of how people in the Edmonton Oiler organization were valued. After winning their first league championship, the owner of the club ordered diamond rings for the players as a token of his appreciation. The size of each diamond received was based on the owner's assessment of the individual's contribution to the team. Trainers and assistant coaches received small stones while Gretzky, the captain, got a big rock. What he found most disturbing was the inconsistency. After several years of being told by the management they were a team, in the end the value of people was based only on their usefulness to the organization. What a different effect it would have had on the team if everyone had received the same size ring!

Affirmation is a deeper form of communication than appreciation. Our words of affirmation to one another can be a catalyst that stimulates growth and development. Authors Gail and Gordon MacDonald say, "Affirmation is that exchange of communication where a person shares with another about the potentials and possibilities he has seen in the other. In a sense, when we affirm others we are believing in their present value and their future potential."[6] *People grow best in an environment in which there are people who believe in them and are not ashamed to communicate that belief.*

There is a profound incident recorded in Matthew's biography of Jesus. In the incident Jesus asks Peter, one of his disciples, 'Who do people say that I am?" After a brief summary of the public opinion polls, Jesus narrows the questioning down. "And who do you say that I am?" Peter boldly asserts, "You are the Christ the Son of the living God." In response Jesus says to Peter, "You are a rock and upon this rock I will build My church."

What an affirmation! I can only imagine how many times Peter later reflected on what Jesus had said to him. Scudder Parker once said, "'People have a way of becoming what you encourage them to be—not what you nag them to be." In other words, people have a way of living up to what other people expect of them.

Mentoring Involves Providing Resources

In addition to making the right assumptions regarding people, the mentoring process also requires providing the necessary resources. Mentors need to be asking their protégés on a consistent basis: "How can I help you reach your goals today?" By sharing resources such as wisdom, information, experience, confidence, insight, or relationships to a protégé, at an appropriate time and manner, the mentor is facilitating development in the other.

Bobb Biehl, President of MasterPlanning Group International defines mentoring as "making the mentor's personal strengths, resources, and network (friendships and contacts) available to help a protégé reach his or her goals."[7] Biehl adds that 80 percent of the "people development process" is simply having the person identify their personal and professional goals and helping them achieve those goals. It is in the latter aspect that providing resources is important. *You never lose when you help people win.*

The first step in enabling people to grow is to assist them in identifying their personal and professional goals. It is impossible to aid people in their development unless they know where they want to grow. Once people have identified the direction they are heading, it can be extremely valuable to meet periodically for the purpose of examining those goals and to provide assistance in any way possible that will result in the achievement of those goals.

In their meetings together, a mentor should encourage the protégé to reflect on his goals and his struggles. Steve was a young man I met in seminary. Upon his graduation he began working as a solo pastor in a church in my area. Steve would often call me up to discuss situations he was struggling with: How do you handle delicate problems? What do you do when people aren't in favor of your ideas? How do you perform a funeral? Steve and I would get together regularly over coffee. We spent considerable time discussing a number of areas, and eventually I was able to ascertain Steve's goals for his church and for his life outside ministry. There were times I provided feedback, other times I simply listened, and on other occasions I provided Steve with material that I had developed or was working on to assist him in his development.

Bobb Biehl has developed a list that I have found to be a valuable tool in assisting other people. When mentoring, I would encourage the mentoree to come with the following:

1. A list of one to three upcoming *decisions* they are facing in which they want some input.

2. A list of one to three *problems* prohibiting them from reaching their goals. Sometimes a mentor can provide resources or reframe the problem so that the protégé looks at the problem from a different vantage point.

3. A list of *plans* that will provide the mentor with general information on the long-range goals of the protégé.

4. A list of *progress points.* All mentors like to know where growth is taking place. This provides the mentor an opportunity to give well deserved praise.

5. A list of *prayer requests* for the mentor's prayer support.

6. Personal *roadblocks,* blind spots, and fears the protégé would like to discuss.

Biehl's model can be a practical tool for those struggling with the pragmatic aspects of what to do when you actually meet. Simply getting together and working through this list would prove incredibly helpful to most protégés. Of course, this should not be perceived as a straight-jacket but as a guideline. Mentors can share wisdom and resources to help their protégés succeed. You never lose when you help other people reach their goals.

Developing an Enriching Relationship

Howard Hendricks, long-time professor at Dallas Seminary, often says, 'You can impress people from a distance but you can only impact them up close." Mentoring involves a relational element. One does not mentor through a lecture in the classroom, through a video cassette, or via a book.

Mentoring involves much more than disseminating information—it requires a relationship. The world is full of people who want to impart what they know by writing a book, by teaching a class, by preaching a sermon, by leading a seminar. Those are all good things. But I can't help get the feeling that while there are many authors, teachers, and preachers in the world, there are sadly too few mentors. For all the thousands who are eager to share their knowledge and skills with others, there are just a handful who are willing to share their lives, who are willing to be transparent, vulnerable, and open about their successes and their failures, their joys and their pain, their faith and their doubts.[9]

Mentoring takes place in a relationship, not a classroom. Barnabas and Paul modeled this concept of relational involvement during their ministry among the Thessalonian believers: 'We loved you so much that we delighted to share with you not only the gospel of God *but our lives as well,* because you had become so dear to us" (I Thess.1: 8). For Paul and Barnabas, assisting others in their growth required an investment of their lives in others.

As part of my doctoral research, I examined the motives of mentors when they give of their time and resources to help younger people develop personally and professionally. One of the primary reasons people cite for acting as mentors is the fact that at some point in their life someone made an investment in them. This desire to want to do something for others is in a sense a repayment. What they inadvertently discover is that life takes on new significance when they involve themselves in the lives of others.

Bob Kraning, who serves as an associate pastor at the First Evangelical Free Church of Fullerton, California, once said: "The ultimate success of my life will not be judged by the number of those who admire me for my accomplishments, but by the number of those who attribute their wholeness to my love for them—by the number of those who have seen their true beauty and worth in my eyes."[10]

There is a beautiful song by Ray Boltz that speaks about what it may be like one day in heaven when we realize the full impact of our investment in the lives of others:

I dreamed I went to heaven
And you were there with me.
We walked upon the streets of gold
Beside the crystal sea.
I heard the angels singing, calling out your name;
You turned and saw this young man
And he was smiling as he came.

He said "Friends, you may not know me now,"
But then he said, "But wait!
You used to teach my Sunday school
When I was only eight,
And every week you would say a prayer
Before the class would start
And one day when you said that prayer
I asked Jesus in my heart."

Chorus
THANK YOU for giving to the Lord,
I am a life that was changed.

THANK YOU for giving to the Lord,
I am so glad you gave.

Then another man stood before you
And said, "Remember the time
A missionary came to your church
And his picture made you cry?
You didn't have much money
But you gave it anyway,
And Jesus took the gift you gave
And that's why I'm here today."

Chorus repeats

One by one they came,
Far as the eye could see;
Each life somehow touched
By your generosity.
Little things that you had done,
Sacrifices made;
Unnoticed on the earth,
In heaven now proclaimed.

And I know up in heaven
You're not supposed to cry,
But I'm almost sure
There was a tear in your eyes
As Jesus took your hand
And you stood before the Lord,
He said, "My child look around you,
Great is your reward."

Chorus repeats.[11]

Action Steps

1. *Think over your life and remember* the individuals who went out of their way to do something special in your life. Identify the different ways these people impacted your life.

2. *Take the time to write* a card of encouragement or affirmation to one person on that list. Express your thanks for the positive impact he or she had on your life.

3. *Take the eulogy test.* When you are dead and gone, how do you want to be remembered? Write down the eulogies you would like given at your funeral, one by each family member, a friend, a work associate, a church member, or someone in your community. Ask yourself: What are you doing today that will live on after your time on earth is over?

4. *Identify two or three people,* probably younger than yourself though not necessarily, that you would like to assist in identifying their goals and investing your time and your resources to help them accomplish those goals.

Ron Lee Davis, who wrote the book *Mentoring: The Strategy of the Master,* presents a helpful checklist for those wanting to seriously accept the challenge of mentoring.[12] Work through the list checking the statements that apply to you:

☐ I am willing to spend the time it takes to build an intensely bonded relationship with the protégé.

☐ I commit myself to believing in the potential and future of the protégé; to telling the learner what kind of exciting future I see ahead for him or her; to visualize and verbalize the possibilities for his or her life.

☐ I am willing to be vulnerable and transparent before the protégé, willing to share not only my strengths and successes, but also my weaknesses, failures, brokenness, and sins.

☐ I am willing to be honest yet affirming in confronting the protégé's errors, faults, and areas of immaturity.

☐ I am committed to standing by the protege through trials—even trials that are self incited as a result of ignorance or error.

☐ I am committed to helping the protégé set goals for his or her spiritual life, career, or ministry, and to helping the protégé dream his or her dream.

☐ I am willing to objectively evaluate the protégé's progress toward his or her goal.

☐ Above all, I am committed to faithfully living out everything I teach.

Notes

[1] Robert H. Schuller, *Tough Times Never Last But Tough People Do.* (New York: Bantam Books, 1984), 199–200.

[2] Ted Engstrom and Norman B. Rohrer, *The Fine Art of Mentoring* (Brentwood, Tenn.: Wolgemuth and Hyatt Publishers, Inc., 1989), 157.

[3] Ron Lee Davis, *Mentoring: The Strategy of the Master.* (Nashville, Tenn.: Thomas Nelson, 1991), 43.

[4] Alan Loy McGinnis, *Bringing Out The Best in People.* (Minneapolis: Augsburg Press).

[5] Dennis Kimbro and Napoleon Hill, *Think and Grow Rich: A Black Choice.* (New York: Fawcett Crest, 1991), 221–223.

[6] Gail and Gordon MacDonald, *If Those Who Read Could Touch.* (Chicago: Moody Press, 1984), 71.

[7] Bobb Biehl, "Mentoring: Finding One Being One." Tape. The Master Planning Group, 1991.

[8] Ibid.

[9] Davis, op. cit., 23.

[10] Ibid, 221.

[11] Ray Boltz, "Thank You" Song

[12] Davis, op.cit., 50–51.

CHAPTER FIVE

YOUR FAMILY

Train up a child in the way he should go.
When he is old, he will not depart from it.
PROVERBS 22:6

It was a magical moment. British athlete Derek Redmond stood behind the starting line in anticipation of winning an Olympic medal at the 1992 Barcelona Games. The gun sounded.

Blasting out of the blocks, 26-year-old Redmond was confident he could win the 400-meter race.

But just a few seconds later, young Derek heard the sound of his right hamstring pop. He went down. Determination etched his face as he attempted to stand. "Get up. Finish," he told himself.

Jim Redmond, Derek's father, was sitting in the stands cheering his son on when he saw what had happened. Seeing his son collapse, Jim bolted from his seat, brushed past the officials and ran to his son's side. Acting like a human crutch, Jim propped up his son as they continued round the oval track. Derek pointed to the finish and together they began to walk. In a race that took the winner only forty-four seconds to complete, Derek, with his father's help, took five minutes. Despite the fact that the race was officially over because the clock had been turned off, the cheer from the crowd grew as they crossed the line together.

When reporters sought their reflections on what transpired, Derek said, 'I finished." His father added, 'I am more proud of him than if he had won."[1]

All parents want to give their children the support that a family life can offer. Parents play a very significant role in the development of their children. Sometimes parenting involves taking care of physical provisions, such as food on the table, suitable clothing and a bed to sleep in; other times it involves providing a place of refuge from the harshness of life; and other times it involves emotional provisions such as love, acceptance, and encouragement. But parenting also involves preparing children for a time when they will face the challenges of life alone. "Good parents" says Dr. Jonas Salk, "Give their children roots and wings. Roots to know where home is, wings to fly away and exercise what's been taught them."

The challenges of being a parent in the '90s is a tough one. The external forces outside the home is only one front on which the battle for effective parenting is being waged. Families also may have to cope with the internal struggles of divorce, abuse, and neglect.

Families on the Fault Line

Statistically the family is not doing well. As part of my teaching responsibilities, I lecture in the field of Family Studies. It is very easy to become pessimistic regarding the family. Some people see very little hope for the long-term survival of the family as we presently know it. Yet within those numbers there are some positive trends. Somewhat smaller in number but no less significant is the phenomenon sweeping across North America—the return and recommitment to family life and family values. Social researchers are discovering that family is still very important to people.

Parents want to be effective parents. Pastor and author John Maxwell's principle regarding the importance of family is this: "Success is having those closest to me, love and respect me the most."[2] Many are indicating they are willing to forgo occupational advancement if it is going to have a detrimental effect on their family. But while parents are desirous to do a good job, they find it stressful to balance the needs of their children with their work and personal needs.

An article in *Fortune* magazine entitled "Why Grade A Executives Get an F as Parents"[3] recognized that many professionals were excelling in the workplace but striking out at home. The author surmised that one of the reasons so many successful professionals fail at home is that to be effective at home requires a different set of skills. In the marketplace the skills that enabled them to succeed included perfectionism, impatience and efficiency. These are not the skills necessary to be effective on the home front.

Author of the bestseller *The Fifth Discipline*, Peter Senge, says, "All the habits that an executive learns in an authoritarian organization are exactly the habits...that make them unsuccessful parents."[4] For many executives having a home life marked by family fun, satisfying family relationships, and healthy kids demands mastering a different skill set.

Unfortunately during the past two decades our society has been consumed by unbridled careerism, where our jobs have become our number one priority and everything has to be in subjection to them. The fallout is the emotional devastation of parents who live with the regrets of misaligned priorities. One father in reflection wrote the following prayer:

A Father's Prayer of Enlightenment

Dear Heavenly Father can you forgive me for hurting my children?

I came from a poor background so I thought that a big house would make my children feel important. I didn't realize that all it takes is my love.

I thought money could bring them happiness, but all it did was make them think that things were more important than people.

I thought spanking would make them tough so that they could defend themselves. All it did was stop me from seeking wisdom so that I could discipline and teach them.

I thought that leaving them alone would make them independent. All it did was force my one son to be the father to my second son.

I thought that by smoothing over all of the family problems I was keeping peace. All I was teaching them was to run rather than lead.

I thought by pretending to be the perfect family in public that I was bringing them respectability. All I was teaching them was to live a lie and keep the secret.

I thought that all I had to do to be a father was make money, stay at home and supply all their material needs. All I taught them was that there is more to being a dad. The problem is they will have to guess what being a dad really is.

And Dear God.
I hope that you can read this prayer. My tears have smudged a lot of words.[5]

Six Qualities of Strong Families

Dr. Nick Stinnett, chairman of the Department of Human Development and the Family at the University of Nebraska, states: "When you have a strong family life, you receive the message that you are loved, cared for and important. The positive intake of love, affection and respect gives you inner resources that help you deal with life more successfully."[6] In the early years of developmental studies on the family, the focus was on the common denominators of dysfunctional families. The assumption was that if we could understand what factors lead to the breakdown of these families we could highlight for parents what not to do. Stinnett and his team of researchers operated with a different reference point. Instead of identifying the commonality among dysfunctional families, they identified the characteristics of healthy families. As Leo Tolstoy said: "All happy families are alike; every unhappy family is unhappy in its own way." Dr. Stinnett concluded that there are six qualities of a strong family:

- The members express appreciation to each other.
- They spend time together.
- They have good family communication.
- They have a spiritual commitment.
- They are able to solve problems in crisis.
- They are committed to the family.[7]

Strong, healthy families are built on strong, supportive foundations. Together, these six qualities form the infrastructure of a strong family.

Developing a Strong Family

Identifying these factors is one thing, but incorporating them into our families is the real challenge. Parents cannot come home one day and announce, "We are going to become more committed." It just doesn't work that way. As Charles Swindoll noted, "Effective family life does not just happen; it's the result of deliberate intention, determination, and practice."[8] Effective parenting requires establishing patterns that lead to strong and enduring families. And while this list of six qualities is not taken directly from Scripture, the Word of God does have a great deal to say about each one.

They express appreciation to each other on a regular basis. William James said, "The deepest principle in human nature is the craving to be appreciated." We all desire to feel as if who we are and what we do makes a difference. The homemaker who chooses to put her professional career on hold to build a family and raise healthy, well-adjusted kids wants to feel that what she is doing is noticed and appreciated. The husband who leaves the home every morning, battles traffic, puts in a full day in an aggressive workplace, and brings home a steady paycheck wants to know that his contribution to the family is noticed and appreciated.

While we find ourselves acknowledging the accuracy of this inner craving, we find ourselves violating this concept routinely. Most of us would agree that we are often more kind to people outside our family than we are to the very people with whom we live. Because of the hectic pace of our daily routines we find ourselves emotionally spent by the end of the day. We want to stop playing the role of being nice to people and we want to kick back and "just be ourselves." We find ourselves slipping into speech patterns marked more by criticism and judgment than mercy and appreciation.

The Apostle Paul indicates the necessity of giving attention to our words. Ephesians 4:29 says, "Let no unwholesome word proceed from your mouth, but only such a word as is good for edification according to the need of the moment, that it may give grace to those who hear." Colossians 4:6 adds, "Let your speech always be with grace, seasoned, as it were, with salt so that you may know how you should respond to each person."

Psychologists are highlighting the harmful impact that speech patterns such as sarcasm, ridicule, and insults can have on other people.

One leading psychologist says it takes nine positive statements to offset every negative judgment a person hears.

While appreciation needs to be a part of every family's vocabulary, there must also be heavy doses of affirmation dispensed as well. Author and pastor Ron Lee Davis says,

> There is an enormous difference between appreciation and affirmation. We appreciate what a person *does*. We affirm who a person is. If all we ever express to our children is appreciation when they have performed well, then they will conclude, consciously or unconsciously, that they are only loved for their achievements and good behavior. This leads to self-doubt and emotional insecurity. Certainly we want to praise and encourage our children when they achieve and succeed. But it is only when we move beyond conditional appreciation to genuine affirmation, whether they are struggling or succeeding, that our children will feel unconditionally and emotionally secure.[9]

A high school buddy of mine, David Kitler, has a tremendous talent for capturing the beauty of wildlife and reproducing it on canvas. He does it so well I have difficulty determining whether it is a picture or a drawing. At age twelve David drew his first picture of an animal, a portrait of the family dog. He drew late one evening when the family was in bed and inadvertently left it on the kitchen table. I'll let Dave explain what happened the next morning:

> I was bent over the sink washing my hair when my mother opened the basement door and called me over to her. She then used a sentence that I can honestly say has been a continual source of comfort, affirmation, confidence building and approval in my life. The words she used were simple, uneducated (she didn't claim to know anything about art) but sincere: "David", she said, "Don't let anyone ever tell you that you are not an artist."

His mother's words of affirmation would play a powerful role in shaping David's life, but it took years for them to come to fruition.

> I couldn't count how many situations I used those encouraging words to get through the tough times. Times when discouragement crept in, times when self-confidence was at a low point and especially those times when I found myself wondering if I

was doing the right thing. As an art teacher I am exposed to a lot of students who have the desire to draw but may be lacking in the confidence to stick with it through the initial trials. knowing how important the words my mother used and the effect they had on me, I don't hold back when it comes to my students. In a vain sort of way I don't care how many of my paintings are hanging on walls when I die, but it would be a great feeling to know that I helped someone the way my mother helped me.

Words can be powerful tools or wicked weapons. In strong families words are used intentionally to express appreciation to one another.

They structure their lives so they can plan time together. One person has described the modern family home as "a domestic cloverleaf on which we pass one another en route to meetings." Obviously one of the often-heard cries of parents is "Not enough time!" Between Mom and Dad working, taxiing kids to and from piano lessons, little league baseball, gymnastics, and the responsibilities of taking care of the home front, there appears too little time to do things together.

According to Virginia Satr (one of the most prominent family therapists) a major problem that families in North America have is that they do not spend enough time together. She says that families are "so fragmented, so busy, so hassled, they end up having a lot of 'half-contacts' with one another...They just make superficial contacts—kind of halfway relating to one another. Communication is not good in this kind of situation because it is hard to communicate with people if you are not spending enough time with them."

Spending time with your children is crucial to your family success. Even the Lord Jesus made sure to spend considerable time with his twelve disciples, so that they would know each other and know Him. Being a successful businessman may take care of your family's financial needs, but it will never replace spending time with them and showing them what a mature Christian is like. In fact, your professional success might get in the way of family communication. Chicago social worker Alice White was quoted as saying, "The parents serve as a model of success, but the kids are afraid they won't get their chance because nobody has shown them how."[10]

For most Christians, there is little or no time for family time. "Most off-work hours are spent trying to catch up with the dozens of family and household tasks that were left undone during the regular work week. When they aren't doing chores, parents guiltily try to do in two days what usually takes seven—that is, to establish a sense of family life for themselves and their children."[11] According to a 1985 University of Maryland study, American parents spend just seventeen hours a week with their children.[12] "The pressures of time, the impoverishment of social life, the anxieties about child care, the fear that children will live in a world of increasing scarcity, the threat of divorce—all these are part of family life today."[13]

Over the past decade the expression, "It is not the quantity of time that one spends with one's family that counts, but the *quality* of time," has been used as a rationalization for not spending enough time with one's family. Dr. Arrnid M. Nicholi, Jr., of Harvard University Medical School, says "time is like oxygen—there's a minimum amount that's necessary for survival. And it takes quantity as well as quality to develop warm and caring relationships."[14] Unfortunately, as United States Senator Dan Coats noted, "Kids don't always have their problems on your quality time. "

Every parent wrestles with priorities when it comes to effective time management. There just is not enough time to do every thing. Paul Lewis in the newsletter *Dad's Only* poses the following questions when establishing time priorities for the upcoming months:

1. What are my child's significant events for which I should save priority time? (ie., birthdays, ball games, recitals, school plays.)

2. What are my child's special needs to which I need to give one-on-one attention? (Birth of a new sibling, problems with a particular teacher or subject, disappointment over not making the team.)

3. How can I best prepare for those special opportunities to share my faith and values with my children? (Family nights, outings, holidays, anniversaries, reunions, helping an elderly neighbor or relative.)[15]

In answering the question "How much time does it take to be a parent?", Paul Lewis says "As much time as you can find. But you're certain to find more if you set priorities, plan ahead, and make the most of life's many small routines. Quality time is simply the sum total of many teachable, intimate, and creative moments you must schedule or which happen unexpectedly."[16]

There can be a tendency to think that if we don't see immediate results, nothing is happening. I once heard of a father who took his son fishing one morning. When they returned home, each wrote about the experience in his diary. The father's entry went like this: "Today I went fishing with Mark. We had nothing but trouble. Our lines constantly got tangled. It was hot. I lost several hooks and one good lure. Ants got into our lunch. And we didn't catch anything. I couldn't wait to get home—what a waste of time." His son wrote in his diary: "Today I went fishing with Dad. We had a wonderful time. In fact, it was the greatest day of my life."

To be sure, most young people would not object to seeing the pendulum swing back in the direction of home. A 1990 special edition of *Time* magazine on the "twenty-something" generation found that 63 percent of the 18-to-29-year-olds polled hoped to spend more time with their children than their parents spent with them.

As Ellen Galinsky of the New York-based Families and Work Institute explains, "These young people have seen their parents come home from work wiped out and not have time for them, and they are saying they don't want to live that way." Not surprisingly, the desire for parental attention and family time is shared by younger children as well. In fact, when fifteen hundred school children were asked "What do you think makes a happy family?" John DeFrain and his colleague Nick Stinnett report that children did not list money, cars, fine homes, or televisions. Instead, the answer most frequently offered was "doing things together."[17] Time is one of the cornerstones of a family's wellbeing.

They deal with crisis in a positive way. Royce Money says, "Even strong families have squabbles and disagreements. But they are able to work through the issues that divide them and keep them from becoming full-blown problems. So the difference between healthy families and failing families is not the presence or absence of conflict, but the way in which the conflict is handled."[18]

In my ten years as a pastor, I encountered a number of families in crisis. I don't claim to understand all the complex dynamics involved, but I do know that it is not the magnitude of the crisis that is of primary concern. Some families have seemingly insurmountable difficulties but find a way to work through them. By comparison, other families have relatively small problems that tear the family apart. The issue is not the presence of problems but how we choose to handle the conflict.

Learn to handle troubles in a positive, constructive way that leads to some type of fair resolution and your family will be strengthened. Talk with your spouse about being honest but remaining positive, focused on the situation or behavior that is the issue, rather than attacking one another. Learn to come to agreements as a family, even if that means working to find a compromise of some kind. A constructive attitude will change the atmosphere of your home from negative and oppressive to positive and supportive.

They affirm religious values. At a time when people say religion is passe, it is somewhat surprising that Stinnet's survey indicated that there is a religious component evident in strong families. There are a number of reasons why this may be so. One is that families with a strong religious orientation share a common value system. A second is that they recognize a power greater than themselves. In his book *Back to the Family*, Dr. Ray Guardendi indicated the emergence of spirituality as a predominant trait in the hundred families he interviewed. Nearly 90 percent of the families in his survey pointed to spirituality as a significant, if not dominant, guiding force in their lives.[19] Responsibilities of parents are outlined in the book of Deuteronomy, which clearly indicates that parents are to give attention to the cultivation, the nurturing of a strong, personalized faith in their children:

> And these words, which I am commanding you today, shall be on your heart; and you shall teach them diligently to your sons and shall talk of them when you sit in your house and when you walk by the way and when you lie down and when you rise up. And you shall bind them as a sign on your hand and they shall be as frontals on your forehead. And you shall write them on the doorposts of your house and on your gates. (Deut.6:4–9)

Faith development in a family is far more than mere attendance on Sunday morning at a place of worship—as important as that is. Christianity is not just adherence to a creed or a body of beliefs. Christianity is a lifestyle. The decision to commit one's life has to make a difference in the way we live our lives.

The Scriptures teach that parents have a number of responsibilities. The Deuteronomy passage recorded above states that part of the parenting mandate involves teaching children the principles and truths of God's word. Complimenting the concept of teaching is that of modeling. Communication theory has evaluated that 7 percent of what a child learns from a parent comes through words, 18 percent from shared experiences and a whopping 75 percent through modeling:

When you thought I wasn't looking, I saw you hang my first painting on the refrigerator, and I wanted to paint another one.

When you thought I wasn't looking, I saw you feed a stray cat, and I thought it was good to be kind to animals.

When you thought I wasn't looking, I saw you make my favorite cake just for me, and I knew that little things are special things.

When you thought I wasn't looking, I heard you say a prayer, and I believed there is a God I could always talk to.

When you thought I wasn't looking, I felt you kiss me goodnight, and I felt loved.

When you thought I wasn't looking, I saw tears come from your eyes, and I learned that sometimes things hurt, but, it's all right to cry.

When you thought I wasn't looking, I saw that you cared, and I wanted to be everything that I could be.

When you thought I wasn't looking, I looked...and wanted to say thanks for all the things I saw when you thought I wasn't looking.[20]

Just as teaching and modeling compliment one another, affirmation and exhortation are two sides of the same coin. By affirming we seek to build up the child, seeking to enhance his or her self-esteem. By exhorting we help them know the right path to follow. There are times in each child's life when correction needs to be provided. Effective parenting demands a form of tough love, but it must be balanced with affirmation.

By cultivating a strong, personalized faith in each member of the family, parents are also contributing to the strengthening of the family unit.

They continually communicate with one another. There is an old adage that goes, "Nothing is as easy as talking, but there is nothing as difficult as communicating." Certainly authentic communication requires adequate amounts of conversation, but conversation does not automatically translate into communication. Families can talk about all sorts of subjects from sports scores to celebrity lives to the great truths of the faith. While information makes up much of a family's conversation, communicating encompasses the transmission of *feelings*.

Strong families are characterized by healthy doses of conversation in which family members discuss things that concern them, events that transpired in their lives, hopes, fears, aspirations, and challenges that each is facing.

Communication involves having the opportunity to talk about information and feelings. It also incorporates the feeling family members experience when they perceive they are being heard. Swiss psychologist and author Paul Tournier warns, "Listen to all the conversations of our world, those between nations as well as those between couples. They are for the most part dialogues of the deaf. Each one speaks primarily to set forth his own ideas, in order to justify himself, in order to enhance himself and to accuse others. Exceedingly few exchanges of viewpoints manifest a real desire to understand the other person."[21]

Parents cannot force communication any more than they can force family members to love each other more. Parents can, however, facilitate it. Openness is something that parents model. Their willingness to disclose to their children age-appropriate things that are going on in the parent's life—issues at work, financial woes, and personal struggles—may provide a platform for family members to share their own thoughts and feelings.

In the Deuteronomy passage referred to earlier, parents are encouraged to make conversation and communication a part of everyday living. Meaningful communication can occur while driving to the store to get milk, while taking the dog for a walk, or while mowing the neighbor's lawn.

In our family, Linda and I have found that one of the best forums for family communication is meal time. That is a natural time for interaction about the activities of each person's day, funny or embarrassing moments, and unusual conversation or occurrences. We have tried to make meal times sacred. We often take the phone off the hook during meal times so that we don't allow other people's agendas to dictate ours. Despite the fact that our children are still relatively small we have had marvelous moments talking about different things.

Bobbie Gee, author of the book *Winning the Image Game,* tells the story of an individual she knew named Al. "As a young man, Al was a skilled artist, a potter. He had a wife and two fine sons. One night his oldest son developed a severe stomachache. Thinking it was only some common intestinal disorder, neither Al nor his wife took the condition seriously. But the malady was actually acute appendicitis, and the boy died suddenly that night.

"Knowing the death could have been prevented if he had only realized the seriousness of the situation, Al's emotional health deteriorated under the enormous burden of his guilt. To make matters worse his wife left him a short time later, leaving him alone with their six-year-old younger son. The hurt and pain of the two situations were more than Al could handle, and he turned to alcohol to help him cope. In time Al became an alcoholic.

"As the alcoholism progressed, Al began to lose everything he possessed—his home, his land, his art objects, everything. Eventually Al died alone in a San Francisco motel room.

"When I heard of Al's death, I reacted with the same disdain this world shows for one who ends his life with nothing material to show for it. 'What a complete failure!' I thought. 'What a totally wasted life!'

As time went by, I began to re-evaluate my earlier harsh judgment. You see, I knew Al's now-adult son, Ernie. He is one of the kindest, most caring, most loving men I have ever known. I watched Ernie with his children and saw the kindness and caring had to come from somewhere.

"I hadn't heard Ernie talk much about his father. It is so hard to defend an alcoholic. One day I worked up my courage to ask him 'I'm really puzzled by something,' I said. 'I know your father was basically the only one to raise you. What on earth did he do that you became such a special person?'"

"Ernie sat quietly and rejected for a few moments. Then he said, 'From my earliest memories as a child until I left home at eighteen, Al came into my room every night, gave me a kiss and said, 'I love you, son.'"

"Tears came to my eyes as I realized what a fool I had been to judge Al as a failure. He had not left any material possessions behind. But he had been a kind, loving father, and he left behind one of the finest, most giving men I have ever known."[22]

They demonstrate a strong commitment to one another. In the nineties nurturing is becoming fashionable. We are seeing a shift toward family concerns. People today are wanting to have a healthy home life. According to recent studies on the state of families in Canada, the Vanier Institute reports that 85 percent of Canadians say that family is an important part of their lives. While people can say that family is a priority, commitment to making a family an enriching social unit involves much more than lip service—it demands commitment.

Commitment to family is more than a decision, it involves an action. "Commitment, like happiness, is more a by-product of other qualities than an end in itself. One cannot simply decide to be 'more committed' to family relationships, the decision must be accompanied by action. It is the development of certain qualities in the family relationship that produces commitment."[23] Raymond Guardendi says that the three key words for every family are *involvement, presence,* and *availability.* These signify a parent's commitment to family success.[24]

Being a parent involves much more than making certain that the physical needs are being met. Effective parenting requires emotional involvement in the child's world. What is going on at school? What challenges are they facing? What is going on in the lives of their friends?

David Kraft was a man who knew the value of a family that was committed to him. David's father was a pastor, a godly influence in the San Francisco bay area. It was a home marked by a strong commitment both to God and to the family. His father constantly, verbally, remembered God's faithfulness in the past so that David might trust God in all his tomorrows. He grew up in love with Jesus, and he himself felt the call of God into pastoral ministry.

David was a big, athletic young man, six-feet-two inches tall, and two hundred pounds. He began working with the Fellowship of Christian Athletes. At the age of thirty-two David was diagnosed as having cancer. It racked his body, and over a period of time his weight dropped to a mere eighty pounds.

When he was about ready to pass from this life into eternity, he asked his father to come into his hospital room. Laying there in the bed, he looked up and said, "'Dad, do you remember when I was a little boy, how you used to just hold me in your arms close to your chest?

His father nodded. Then David asked, "'Do you think, Dad, you could do that one more time? One last time?" Again his father nodded. He bent down to pick up his son and held him close to his chest, so that his son's face was right next to his father's. Tears were streaming down both faces. The son said simply, "Thank you for building the kind of character into my life that can enable me to face a moment like this."[25]

I suspect it is the experience of many that family relationships provide our greatest heartaches. At the same time, they also provide our greatest joy. Study after study reveals an overwhelming agreement that, for the vast majority of us, the family constitutes our greatest support and resource system, and our major source of pleasure and satisfaction in life.

Action Steps

1. *Place the list of six qualities* that compose a strong family in a visible place in your home. Let it provide a gentle reminder to you each day of the qualities of a happy family.

2. *Develop your skills* in each of these six areas. Focus on one quality each week, making it the theme of your devotions. Ask your mate to provide feedback and some helpful suggestions for improving your abilities.

3. *Consider becoming a participant* in a family enrichment program. Numerous churches and community groups offer short term programs. Your communications skills may not require a major overhaul, but making some minor adjustments can lead to profound changes in your family life.

Notes

[1] *USA Today*, 4 August 1992

[2] John Maxwell, Tape—Pastors Conference, Hunstville, Ontario, Summer 1990.

[3] "Why Grade A Executive Get an F as Parents" *Fortune*, January 1990, 36–46.

[4] Peter M. Senge, *The Fifth Discipline*. (New York: Doubleday Currency, 1990), 312.

[5] John Ellis, *Regina Leader Post,* 28 February 1994.

[6] Nick Stinnett, *USA Today,* 28 January 1986.

[7] Stinnett's work was the basis for George Rekers, *Family Building: Six Qualities of Strong Families.* (Ventura, Calif.: RegalBooks, 1985).

[8] Charles Swindoll, *Growing Wise in Family Life.* (Portland, Oreg.: Multnomah Press, 1988),

[9] Ron Lee Davis, *Mentoring: The Strategy of the Master.* (Nashville, Tenn.: Thomas Nelson, 1991), 193.

[10] Lillian B. Rubin, *Families on the Fault Line: America's Working Class Speaks About the Family, the Economy, and Ethnicity.* (New York: HarperCollins Publishers, 1994), 44.

[11] Ibid, 97.

[12] Kenneth Labich, "Can Your Career Hurt Your Kids?" *Fortune,* 20 May 1991.

[13] Rubin, op. cit., 98.

[14] Quoted in George Rekers, *Family Building: Six Qualities of Strong Families.* (Ventura, Calif.: RegalBooks, 1985), 53.

[15] Paul Lewis, *Dad's Only.* 1993.

[16] Ibid.

[17] William R Mattox, Jr. "Two Career Parents Spend Too Little Time with the Family" in *Family in America: opposing viewpoints.* (San Diego: Greenhaven Press, 1992), 189.

[18] Royce Money, Building *Stronger Families: Family Enrichment in the Home, Church and Community.* (Wheaton, Ill.: Victor Books, 1984), 25.

[19] Raymond N. Guardendi, *Back to the Family: Proven Advice on Building a Stronger, Healthier, Happier Family.* NewYork: Fireside, 1991).

[20] David Walls, *Learning to Love When Love Isn't Easy.* (Wheaton, Ill.: Victor Books, 1992) 42.

[21] Paul Tournier, *To Understand Each Other.* (Louisville, Ky.: John Knox Press, 1972), 8–9.

[22] Bobbi Gee in *Chicken Soup for the Soul,* ed. Jack Canfield and Mark Hansen, (Deerfield, Fla.: Health Communications, 1993), 117–118.

[23] Money, op. cit., 56.

[24] Guardendi op. cit.

[25] Ron Lee Davis, "Introducing Your Child to Christ", *Preaching Today,* Tape 92.

CHAPTER SIX

YOUR SPOUSE

Getting married is easy.
Staying married is more difficult.
Staying happily married for a lifetime would
be considered among the fine arts.

AUTHOR UNKNOWN

The story is told of a former mayor of Philadelphia taking his wife out for dinner one evening. He stopped at a local service station to get some gas, and while the attendant began filling the gas tank, the mayor went inside to purchase a couple of small items. When he returned the gas station attendant was involved in a conversation with his wife through the open window. After he paid for the gas, the mayor inquired as to whether his wife knew the gas station attendant. "Yes," she said, "We used to date when we were in high school."

The mayor found this revelation intriguing and said to his wife, "You know, sweetheart, if you married him instead of me you would be married to a gas station attendant."

She took no time in setting the record straight: "That's not true, dear. If I married him instead of you, he would be the mayor of Philadelphia!"

Who you choose to marry is one of the most important decisions that you will make. Regardless of your occupation, your spouse will have a profound impact on your effectiveness. Many pastors and business executives have confessed that a spouse is the "make-it-or-break-it" link in their professional effectiveness. "Yet ironically, when we choose a mate, we don't concern ourselves with whether that person has the potential to support us in our life and career," notes sociologist Michael Zey.[1]

Solomon's admonition to "rejoice in the wife of your youth" (Prov. 5:17) appears out of step with a society that is characterized by disposable relationships. It is interesting to note that Solomon admonishes a man not only to rejoice in his wife, but in the wife of his youth, implying the woman that he married when he was young—his "first choice," so to speak.

With a divorce rate that has quadrupled in the past thirty years, many obviously do not heed Solomon's advice. The marital trend of the nineties is a series of monogamous relationships. With the fear of AIDS and other sexually transmitted diseases, adults today are thinking twice about extramarital affairs. They are, however, still going from one relationship to another.

Such is the story of Dan and Brenda. The couple met and married when they were attending college. Brenda chose to postpone her academic pursuits and went to work to keep them afloat. After college came three years of seminary for Dan. Although two kids were added to their family, she continued to be the breadwinner. With seminary behind them, Dan was accepted into a Ph.D. program at a very prestigious university on the East Coast. Again Brenda assumed responsibility for putting food on the table. She did so willingly. She loved her husband and was willing to do whatever it took to see Dan in a career that he wanted desperately to pursue. The long-anticipated graduation arrived, followed by a lucrative offer at a major Canadian university. It was what the couple wanted. However, the dream quickly dissipated. Within nine months of accepting the position, Dan left her and the kids, and he moved into an apartment with one of his female students. How could a Christian man act in that way? What could cause that kind of relational destruction?

Unfortunately, that story—while true—is not unique. The circumstances may vary but the trend is increasing. The relationship continues as long as it is mutually beneficial, but once one partner no longer seems to need the other, as Dan thought he no longer needed Brenda, the marriage contract is terminated. It has outlived its usefulness. Regardless of the particulars, most divorces are caused by an inordinate degree of selfishness.

Drifting Marriages

Not all marriages terminate amidst scandalous affairs, heated skirmishes, or abusive behaviors. They don't all end in big blow-outs. Some collapse as a result of slow leaks. The people in them neglected to build intimacy. This drifting apart can be seen in what one clever observer of marriage called "The Seven Stages of the Married Cold."

The first year he says; "Honey, I'm worried about my sweetheart. You've got a bad sniffle and there's no telling about these things with all this strep around. I'm taking you to the clinic right now for a checkup."

The second year, he says: "Listen, darling, I don't like the sound of that cough. I've called Doc Miller to rush over here. Now go to bed and get some rest. Please, do it for your honey."

The third year, he says: "Maybe you had better lie down, sweetheart. Nothing like a little rest when you feel punk. I'll bring you something to eat. Do we have any soup?"

The fourth year, he says: "Look, dear, be sensible. After you feed the kids and get the dishes washed, you'd better hit the sack."

The fifth year, he says: "Why don't you get yourself a couple of aspirin?"

The sixth year, he says: "If you'd just gargle or something instead of sitting around barking like a seal, I would appreciate it."

The seventh year, he says, "For Pete's sake, stop sneezing! What are you trying to do, give me pneumonia?"[2]

Leo Buscaglia is one of the best known speakers on the topic of relationships. He made this astute observation: "Love never dies a natural death. It dies from neglect and abandonment. It dies of blindness and indifference and of being taken for granted. Things omitted are often more deadly than errors committed. In the end love dies of weariness, from not being nurtured. We don't really fall out of love any more than we fall into it. When love dies, one or both partners have neglected it, have failed to replenish and renew it. Like any other living, growing thing, love requires effort to keep it healthy."[3]

Anyone who has gone fishing in a boat knows the subtlety of drifting. Once you and your fishing party have your gear in the boat, you settle for a place on the lake where you think the fish are biting. While enjoying the great outdoors and the excitement of a nibble, then a bite, followed by the challenge of reeling in the "big one," you become almost oblivious to the fact that the boat has drifted significantly from your original location. In fact you may have drifted a mile or two from where you started, barely noticing the subtle shifts.

Randy and Cynthia didn't notice their drifting. Randy was the quintessential businessman in pursuit of his life-long dream: heading to his corporate office every day in a three-piece suit while spending every weekend tending to his acreage at the edge of the city. Randy's wife, Cynthia, a gifted writer and capable administrator, had put her career on hold for ten years while raising the three children. They had met years earlier when she was his administrative assistant. He was captivated by her charm, her social confidence and her pleasing-to-the-eyes beauty. She was enamored by his quiet confidence, his capable leadership and his emotional stability so lacking in her childhood home.

Randy had made a number of sacrifices while scaling the corporate ladder. His marriage and his kids had made even greater sacrifices. His job in a multinational organization required frequent traveling. Randy loved the pace and the adventure. The opportunities for advancement looked endless. While everything was going well on the business front, things were less than ideal at home.

Randy was not content with success in the business arena, he also wanted to carry on the family tradition of having a ranch and taking care of the herd on weekends. Some poor business decisions in the early years put Randy and Cynthia under tremendous financial strain. However, the real issue was not the poor decisions. According to Cynthia, it was the way the decisions were made—unilaterally and without any mutual discussion. This unsettled issue was left untended, like a smoldering fire. When the kids were older, Cynthia secured a job in a major marketing firm. Because of the lack of trust in financial matters, Cynthia refused to allow any of her money to be spent repaying the debts occurred from earlier, costly and foolish decisions.

With the kids more independent, Cynthia began to examine the strained relationship between herself and Randy. His preoccupation with his career, his lack of interest in deeper levels of meaningful conversation and his inability to express his feelings were the reasons Cynthia began to question what future their relationship had. Several months later, she moved out, taking two of their three children with her. She thought it was better than living in the shell of a hollow marriage.

Dr. Donald Harvey, in his book *The Drifting Marriage*, notes that this principle of drifting is the most common form of marital failure— and also the most dangerous. "It is subtle. It is quiet. It is non-offensive. It sounds no alarms. It just gradually creeps into our lives. And then it destroys."[4]

The Wall

Their wedding picture mocked them from the table, these two
whose minds no longer touched each other.

They lived with such a heavy barricade between them
that neither battering ram of words
nor artilleries of touch could break it down.

Somewhere, between the oldest child's first tooth
and the youngest daughter's graduation,
they lost each other.

Throughout the years each slowly unraveled
that tangled ball of string called self,
and as they tugged at stubborn knots,
each hid his searching from the other.

Sometimes she cried at night
and begged the whispering darkness to tell her who she was.
He lay beside her, snoring like a hibernating bear,
unaware of her winter.

Once, after they had made love,
he wanted to tell her how afraid he was of dying,
but, fearing to show his naked soul,
he spoke instead about the beauty of her breasts.

She took a course on modern art,
trying to find herself in colors splashed upon a canvas,
complaining to other women about men who are insensitive.

He climbed into a tomb called "The Office,"
wrapped his mind in a shroud of paper figures,
and buried himself in customers.

Slowly, the wall between them rose, cemented by the mortar of
indifference.

One day, reaching out to touch each other
they found a barrier they could not penetrate,
and recoiling from the coldness of the stone,
each retreated from the stranger on the other side.

For when loves dies, it is not in a moment of angry battle,
nor when fiery bodies lose their heat.
It lies panting, exhausted
expiring at the bottom of a wall it could not scale.

Author Unknown

On the outside everything appears to be in order. There is a certain
degree of contentment. The changes that occur are barely visible at first.
Each person in the marriage is changing; life has a way of forcing them
to do that. But instead of growing together, people find their marriages
growing apart.

There are any number of reasons to explain why the shifting occurs.
Three of the most common are *unrealistic expectations coming into a
marriage, the busyness of people's lives that hinders communication,* and the
inability to both understand and adjust to the "seasons" of marriage.

Unrealistic expectations

In part, marital drifting begins with the expectations that people
bring into a marriage. Author and Pastor Doug Murren, in assessing the
statistic that 50 percent of today's marriages will end in divorce, says the
reason is "…not because they devalue marriage, but because they expect
so much from it."[5]

These unrealistic expectations may be in the area of standard of living, career status, or the size of your family. Certainly the primary expectation people have when entering a marriage is that the marriage will
make them happy. No one enters into a marriage to become miserable.
"The happiness we hope for in marriage is a catchall word that embraces
many spoken and unspoken wishes for fulfillment…Many people turn
to marriage hoping to find ultimate happiness and grace for their lives.
Some find a pot of gold, others face disillusionment."[6]

Erich Fromm, in his book *The Art of Loving*, says, "This attitude—that nothing is as easy as love—has continued to be the prevalent idea about love in spite of the overwhelming evidence to the contrary. There is hardly any activity, any enterprise, which is started with such tremendous hopes and expectations, and yet, which fails so regularly as love." In a previous generation when a marriage did not live up to its advance billing, people stuck it out. Divorce was not an option. Certainly that attitude has changed. People are in search of self-fulfillment. The marriage union exists to meet one's needs and desires and it will survive "as long as we both shall love."

Part of the difficulty is that the partner, the other person in your marriage, is expected to meet needs that he/she is incapable of fulfilling. The Bible indicates that humankind was created with two levels of intimacy. One is relational intimacy with our creator God. This is the relationship that meets our inner longing for purpose, for meaning in our lives. The other is on a human level. When God created the earth, He Himself declared it is not good for man to be alone. As a result of that relational vacuum, God created woman.

Without trying to oversimplify the complexity of human relationships, I would suggest that some people expect their marriage to fulfill both levels of intimacy. Unfortunately, a spouse cannot meet both. This need for another level of intimacy gets expressed with a gnawing sense of dissatisfaction. "I love you but I'm still not happy," or "There must be more to life that just this."

The reality is that no one can *make* us happy. People *choose* to be happy. It is naive to think that two unhappy people can come together in a marriage union and expect to have a happy marriage. It doesn't work that way. Yet many people pursue marriage because they live under the false illusion that their mate's sole purpose is to make them happy. Happiness is an inside job. A marriage partner can add to your happiness, but he or she cannot make you happy.

Too Busy for Intimacy

Another reason why marriages may slowly drift apart is that they allow the busyness of life to crowd out the cultivation of intimacy. The shifts that take place in a marriage are subtle at first. Husbands can become preoccupied with establishing or advancing their careers.

One evening I heard Pat Williams give his testimony. Pat is the general manager of the NBA's Orlando Magic basketball team. What captivated my interest in Pat's story is that I could identify with his thinking. While he was dating his soon-to-be wife, Pat had worked hard at romancing her, putting his best foot forward. As soon as he got married, he resumed his attention on his job. In his mind he was thinking, 'I need to get this relational dimension in order so that I can move on to other things." Many men can identify with that line of thinking. Unfortunately a marriage is not something static. It is designed to be a dynamic relationship. It took years for Pat to recognize the mistakes he had made in his marriage and to rectify them. It meant changing not just his approach to his job, but his ideas about what is important in life.

Husbands are not the only ones who are preoccupied. Career advancement and rearing children can consume a woman's time and attention, leaving little for her husband. Whatever the stated reasons, dual-career marriages have become the norm in our society. Sixty-five percent of American families are dual-income homes. They present special challenges.

The pressures of juggling the demands of work with home lead both partners to near exhaustion. Tension and anger are commonplace. In her study of dual-career families, Lilian Rubian observed: "The women, exhausted from doing two days' work in one, angry at the need to assume obligations without corresponding entitlements, push their men in ways unknown before. The men, battered by economic uncertainty and by the escalating demands of their wives, feel embattled and victimized on two fronts—one outside the home, the other inside. Consequently, when their wives seem not to see the family work they do, when they don't acknowledge and credit it, when they fail to appreciate them, the men feel violated and betrayed."[7] Learning to take time for each other is crucial for your marriage to succeed.

The Seasons of a Marriage

Marriages change. Families change. God designed both marriage and family to be dynamic, ever changing, not static. As popular author Walter Trobisch says, "Marriage is not an achievement which is finished. It is a dynamic process between two people, a relation which is constantly being changed, which grows or dies."[8] The changes that are forced upon the marriage may come from a number of forces: the arrival of children, the demands of getting a career started, physical changes for both the male and the female, mid-life crises, the empty-nest syndrome, and aging issues. Any one of these has the ability to significantly impact the quality of one's marriage.

Couples must adapt to the changes that are occurring within the individual and within the relationship. Some view change as a threat. By understanding the various seasons of a marriage, one can adapt to the unique challenges of each stage.

Tragically, during the empty-nest period, when the last child leaves home, a significant number of couples divorce. For years, the glue that kept the couple together was the children, and now that the children have moved away all that remains is the emptiness of a very shallow marriage. This issue of a hollow marriage is a result of many years of neglect. The couple ignored or failed to confront the basics that are necessary for the cultivation of intimacy. Not wanting to address the issues while the children were at home, they chose to live lives of quiet desperation. If they don't get a divorce, too many "succumb to a form of apathy or dull but tolerable coexistence: a kind of death-in-life."[9]

If couples understood that there may be periods in a marriage where everything is not going to go smoothly and if they are willing to make the effort to continue to work at their relationships, many couples attest to the fact that a marriage can survive. Couples who determine to expect to stay together forever say their attitude is directly responsible for their ability to work through the tough times.

Commitment in a marriage context is being re-examined in the '90s. There was a time when commitment in marriage was associated with confinement, suffocation, predictability, and loss of self. But divorce has its implications, too. A recent study of people who were divorced and now remarried asked, "If you knew then what you know now about relationships, would you have stayed married to your first partner?" A significant number said yes. These couples came to the realization that when one divorces and remarries he or she is simply trading one set of problems for a new set of problems.

According to psychologists Lonnie Barbach and David Geisinger, "Commitment involves both an investment and a promise: an investment of energies, thoughts, patience, feelings, and time, along with a promise to protect the relationship from harm and to remain in it to solve any issues that arise."

They add, "Making a commitment means that your *intention* is to *make* the relationship work; it does not mean waiting and seeing *if* it will work. It is an active, not a passive stance, and it is exemplified by the willingness to continue working on problems until some satisfactory resolution can be reached, even if for a time there is no solution in sight."[10]

Yale psychologist Robert Sternberg believes that with such effort there is hope. "'Living happily ever after' need not be a myth, but if it is to be a reality, the happiness must be based upon different configurations of mutual feelings and various times in a relationship. Couples who expect their passion to last forever, or their intimacy to remain unchallenged, are in for a disappointment...We must constantly work at understanding, building and rebuilding our loving relationships."[11]

Going the Distance

Most of life's meaningful accomplishments are achieved over time and though tenacity, and this is particularly true if your goal is to sustain a vibrant, long-term relationship. Anything of lasting value does not come easy. It takes time, commitment and a willingness to meet your mate's needs.

Christian psychologist Dr. William Harley has written a helpful book entitled *His Needs, Her Needs*.[12] In it he lists five basic needs men expect their wives to meet and five needs women want their husbands to fulfill. He suggests that the way to keep the vibrancy of the marriage alive is to make certain that each partner is mindful of and working diligently to meet the needs of one's partner.

His Needs	Her Needs
1. Sexual fulfillment	1. Affection
2. Recreational companionship	2. Conversation
3. An attractive spouse	3. Honesty and openness
4. Domestic support	4. Financial support
5. Admiration	5. Family commitment

The old adage "the grass is always greener on the other side of the fence" needs qualification. The truth is, the grass is greener where it is watered. The best defense against marital failure is giving the marriage the time and attention that it needs and deserves. "If I have learned anything at all in dealing with these relationships that are on the verge of breaking up, it is this: no one leaves a healthy marriage."[13]

Action Steps

1. *Spend time together.* In a 1986 *Psychology Today* survey three hundred couples were asked what kept them together. One of the major "staying factors" was simply "time spent together."

2. *Work at meeting each others' needs.* Marriage, as the Bible defines it, was not meant to be a 50/50 proposition. It was designed to be a 100 percent proposition on the part of both partners. Refer to the list of "His Needs and Her Needs" and select one of the five needs mentioned. Focus on meeting that need for your spouse on a consistent basis. All five are important, but focus on enhancing your effectiveness in one area.

3. *Have periodic "State of the Marriage" meetings.* One of the things I notice about relationships on our college campus is the strong desire of couples to talk about the relationship. It is important for each of them to know where he or she stands. How does the other person feel about the relationship? Where does each see the relationship going? What would each like to see happen? While there are obvious differences between a marriage and a dating situation, there still remains the desire to periodically discuss the marriage relationship. Take the time one evening to get alone and evaluate the state of your marriage.

Notes

[1] Michael G. Zey, *Winning With People: Building Lifelong Professional and Personal Success Through the Supporting Cast Principle.* (Los Angles: Jeremy P. Tarcher, 1990), 154.

[2] Dennis Rainey, *Lonely Husbands, Lonely Wives.* (Dallas: Word Publishers, 1989), 5–6.

[3] Leo Buscaglia, *Born to Love: reflections on loving.* (Thorfare, N.J.: Slack Inc., 1992), 6.

[4] Donald R Harvey, *The Drifting Marriage.* (Old Tappan, N.J.: Fleming H. Revell, 1988), 11.

[5] Doug Murren and Barb Shurin, *Is It Real When It Doesn't Work?* (Nashville, Tenn.: Thomas Nelson Publishers, 1990), 130.

[6] Thomas Moore, *Soul Mates: Honoring the Mysteries of Love and Relationship.* (New York: Harper-Collins, 1994), 49–50

[7] Lillian Rubian, *Families on the Fault Line.* (New York: Harper-Collins Publishers, 1994), 87–88.

[8] Walter Trobisch quoted in *Marriage Partnership,* Winter 1989, 17.

[9] Lonnie Barbach, and David Geisinger, *Going the Distance: Secrets to Lifelong Love,* (New York: Doubleday, 1991), viii.

[10] Ibid, 185.

[11] Sternberg quoted in David G. Myers *The Pursuit of Happiness.* (New York: William Morrow, 1992), 175.

[12] William F. Harley, Jr. *His Needs, Her Needs.* (Old Tappan, N.J.: Fleming H. Revel Company, 1986).

[13] Harvey, op. cit., 166.

CHAPTER SEVEN

YOUR WINNING TEAM

Never underestimate the power of a committed group of people to change the world. In fact, it is the only thing that ever has.
MARGARET MEAD

Organizations and individuals in the '90s are understanding that the essence of success is teamwork. More and more people are working in teams. There is a definite shift from an emphasis on individual effort to an emphasis on collective effort. Whether it be in ministry, business, politics, or athletics, the ability to be a vital component of a dynamic team is an essential skill.

"Teams are everywhere," says consultant and author Glenn Parker. "In business we have new product teams, quality teams, and project teams. In sports we have offensive teams, defensive teams, first teams, second teams, special teams, and all-star teams. In the arts a team is referred to in a variety of ways, including cast, crew, ensemble, company, and troupe. In politics we have party, caucus, committee, and council."[1] In ministry circles today we have pastoral teams, ministry teams, evangelism teams, drama teams and worship teams.

Being a part of a team involves developing certain relational skills. The principles and practices we utilize in peer relationships differ significantly from those we use in relating to our family, mentors, prótegés or friends.

Since so much of our adult lives revolves around work, the relational concepts outlined in this book have significant implications for work-related relationships. Most Christian adults that I know want to be successful in their jobs. Most are interested in succeeding in the market-place and handling more responsibility than usually comes with entry-level positions. To do so in our changing business structure demands possessing a strong set of relational skills, including the ability to work on a team and be a team player.

"Although many of us like to think we are self-sufficient, can-do-it-all people, most of us are actually very limited in what we can accomplish strictly on our own. Many of us are secretly frustrated by our inability to do it all ourselves."[2]

A Workplace Revolution

Teamwork is how things get done in the '90s. More than 50 percent of all Fortune 500 companies now utilize some form of self-directed work teams, and it is estimated that by the year 2000, 90 percent of North American organizations will have at least some self-directed work teams. Following the self-centered, dog-eat-dog mentality of the '70s and '80s, there is a resurgence of interest in teamwork. The change in the way organizations are structured it demands that people who are going to be effective in the changing economy must be people who are team players.

Business offices are not the only places where teamwork is important. Many North American pastors are still struggling with the ability to work with people. A 1988 study among Southern Baptists found that more than two thousand pastors were fired by their churches during an eighteen-month period, 116 each month, a 31 percent increase over the rate found in the 1984 study. About half of the ousted pastors leave the ministry and go into other kinds of work.

James Means notes,

The top reason cited for forced terminations in pastoral ministry is relational problems between the pastor and lay leaders... the most basic cause of ineffectiveness and failure is an inability to build and sustain meaningful collegial relationships with the church's lay leadership. Many pastors simply do not realize the pivotal importance of relationships.[4]

Transitioning from individual recognition to team recognition is not easy. This is, in part, why pastoral leaders have a difficult time making the transition from pre-service training (i.e., Bible college or seminary) to actual church ministry. The skills needed to thrive in the educational environment are solely based on individual achievement. Education is oriented toward the individual and his or her ability to master the course content. Conversely, in a ministry context one's effectiveness is not based primarily on individual recognition but on one's ability to "equip the saints to do the work of ministry" (Eph. 4: 7–11).

This truth is also evident in business. Jeffrey Pfeffer maintains that we must unlearn this notion that life is a matter of individual effort, ability, and achievement. "Individual success in organizations is quite frequently a matter of working with and through other people, and organizational success is often a function of how successfully individuals can coordinate their activities."[5]

Being a member of a dynamic team is an exhilarating experience. I had the opportunity to serve on the pastoral teams of two very large churches. One situation was electrifying. It demonstrated many of the qualities of excellent teams: common direction, mutual encouragement, and an attitude of doing whatever it takes to be effective. Whenever staff members wanted to introduce a new initiative, other staff members provided insights, recommendations, and encouragement. Periodically team members found themselves snowed under by the task of ministry. On those occasions, others stepped in and provided assistance. There was chemistry on this team that was evident in weekly staff meetings, on the golf course, and at staff social functions. Whenever criticism of staff members began to surface, other staff members were quick to defend, to make certain the facts of the situation were cast in their proper light. Whenever a situation demanded confrontation, it occurred in private and with an attitude of support.

What I appreciated most about this experience was the balanced emphasis involving supportive relationships as well as productive results. Authors Douglass and Douglass say these two aspects have to work in tandem for a team experience to be a positive one. "There is a synergy between the two, and we have to keep them in balance. There has been too much emphasis on results, often at the expense of relationships. Teams that hope to survive and thrive must be more sensitive to this balance."[6]

My other team experience that was not as stimulating. It was characterized more by hidden agendas, turf wars, and suspicion, rather than by common goals, synergy and trust. Several of the team members had different visions that they were pursuing. No common strategy was implemented that provided needed direction and focus.

At one staff meeting in particular, I can recall being broadsided by an issue that could have been better dealt with privately on a one-on-one basis. On this particular occasion, one of the team members questioned me on what he perceived was an "end-run"—not following the proper procedure. As a result, he questioned my loyalty to the rest of the pastoral team. The person used the staff meeting as a platform to express his displeasure while getting maximum impact in a group, rather than an individual, setting. With a simple rehearsal of the facts, I was able to clarify my position and set the record straight. Unfortunately, this was not an isolated incident but more indicative of a general pattern of relating. Needless to say those kind of behaviors don't lend themselves to strong team play.

Teamwork in Scripture

Teamwork is not a new concept. There are many examples of teams and teamwork in Scripture. The ancient wisdom of Solomon noted,

> Two are better than one, because they have a good reward for their labor. If one falls down, his friend can pick him up. But pity the man who falls and has no one to help him up!...Though one may be overpowered, two can defend themselves. A chord of three strands is not quickly broken. (Eccles. 4:9–12)

A modern paraphrase of the relational principle outlined in this passage is "the whole is greater than the sum of its parts," or, as I like to say, "With people, one plus one equals more than two." Obviously the text has a broader application than workplace considerations. But it does highlight the tremendous value of shifting one's focus from individual achievement to team effort.

A variety of other examples of team work are portrayed in Scripture. Jesus and his team of disciples is an obvious example. Christ took twelve men from different parts of society and created a force that would change the world.

King David's supporting cast included many great warriors, valiant men, and giant killers. David's success was not due to individual achievement alone; much credit went to his mighty men (and David's wisdom in relying upon them).

Another group of men highlighted in Scripture is that of Nehemiah and his team. The book of Nehemiah provides a detailed description of teamwork. It identifies the formation, development and deployment of this team and its accomplishments. God had placed on Nehemiah's heart a burden to rebuild the ruined walls of Jerusalem. By rebuilding the walls the people would have a place to live and the people would take pride in their homeland again. But Nehemiah knew that the task of rebuilding would demand much more than he could do alone.

The Dynamics of Team Building

Nehemiah knew the value of peer relationships and working in a team environment. The team experience has been defined this way:

T- Together

E - Everyone

A - Achieves

M- More

While effective teams come in different sizes, they often share common characteristics: *a shared vision, a common strategy, open lines of communication, relational involvement and a willingness to sacrifice.*

A shared vision

One of the distinguishing characteristics that sets a team apart from a committee is a common vision. According to Ralph Stayer, CEO of Johnsonville Foods: "A team has a vision. Committees have agendas— often, separate agendas."

Nehemiah understood the magnetic power of a shared vision, both in terms of rebuilding the wall and more importantly in helping the Jewish people come together as a united nation. The city of Jerusalem had been captured and much of it destroyed. Wile serving as a cupbearer to the king of Persia, Nehemiah had a vision of Jerusalem rebuilt with strong walls as a testimony to the glory of God. His mission was to translate that vision into action.

One of the first things Nehemiah did, after surveying the ruins of his city, was mobilize the people who were living there. The way that Nehemiah did this was to have the team embrace a common vision: "Then I said to them, 'You see the trouble we are in: Jerusalem lies in ruins, and its gates have been burned with fire. Come, let us rebuild the wall of Jerusalem, and we will no longer be in disgrace'" (Neh. 2:17).

Having a vision is critical for three major reasons. *First, it provides direction.* It is a road map orienting people to their destination. People often think in terms of in developing ministries—planning, training, programming, and staffing—with very little attention given to asking, 'What do we want to accomplish?"

Second, a vision provides motivation, an emotional catalyst to activity. Effective visions are inspiring when they touch the emotions. Martin Luther King, Jr.'s 'I have a dream" speech was a vision that stirred emotions during the civil rights era, and it continues to arouse them thirty years later. By focusing on a vision, as Bennis and Nanus point out, the leader appeals to the "emotional and spiritual resources of the group; its values, commitment and aspirations." The manager, by contrast, focuses on the "physical resources of the group—on the budget, human skills, physical resources and organizational structure."[7]

Third, an effective vision attracts people. Too often those in charge of organizations attempt to push people into positions in order to fulfill their own goals and objectives. Rather than attracting others through an inspiring vision, they want to own and make a reality. It is more commonly *the idea* that unites people in a common effort, not the charisma of the leader. As Bennis and Nanus have noted, such a vision "may be as vague as a dream or as precise as a goal or mission statement."[9] Regardless of its form, it must be one that is personal to the team. The vision must capture the imagination and sustain team members beyond the endless activities that are a part of everyone's job description—committee meetings, recruitment, training, planning, organizing people, schedules and facilities.

While the responsibility of formulating a vision cannot be delegated, the leader may choose to include others in the process. When my former church was faced with a singles' ministry that no longer met the group's needs, we pulled together key people, both single and newly married couples, to address the needs as well as to lay out a strategy to meet them. After much discussion this core formulated a mission statement describing what they desired to see God do. The process also involved envisioning what our group would look like if our intentions became reality. The vision, in this case a specific mission statement, became the catalyst for turning a struggling, disheartened group of 20–25 into a vibrant and dynamic community that quickly attracted young adults, with increased attendance ranging from 75–120.

A common strategy

A shared vision demands a common strategy. Once the vision has been articulated, it is then necessary to formulate the strategy to achieve the desired outcome. While rarely is an organization restricted to only one way to accomplish a goal, a strategic approach must be determined and communicated.

Every organization has a strategy. It may not be effective, it may not even be articulated, but every organization has one. It is evidenced in the way weekly decisions are made. The key to success is to formulate and articulate a long-range framework aimed at creating a united effort. It should allow all those involved in the program to know their areas of responsibility. Providing such a framework enhances weekly decision-making and provides a sense of direction.

Let's face it, there are several ways of building a wall. But to make it secure, everyone must work off the same set of blueprints. In chapter three of his book, Nehemiah outlines the specific responsibilities that each team had to fulfill to manage the Sheep gate, the Fish Gate, the Jeshanah Gate, the Valley Gate, the Dung Gate, the Fountain Gate and the Horse Gate.

People consistently confuse strategy with the planning process. When asked about strategy, coordinators of programs quickly remark, "We have planning meetings every quarter."

Strategy and planning may on occasion overlap, but they are not synonymous. Using an analogy from sports, the difference between a strategy and the planning process is the difference between a game plan and a huddle. Before every game the coaching staff drafts a game plan. Seeking to maximize their strengths, they outline how they are going to approach the game in order to achieve their goal, which, ultimately, is to win the game. Every member of the team is made thoroughly aware of the game plan.

Unless things go disastrously wrong, the game plan will remain constant. But at various points in the game, certain members of the team congregate in huddles and plan specific plays consistent with the game plan. The function of the huddle is to devise short-term steps to accomplish the goal and to allow individuals on the field to coordinate their efforts.

In the same way, it is essential for an organization or a team to formulate one overall strategy to facilitate the transforming of the vision into reality. At various stages planning will be required to unite the efforts and to see that each person carries out his or her responsibility.

Open lines of communication

George Bernard Shaw once said, "The greatest problem of communication is the illusion that it has been accomplished." The effectiveness of a team is also based on its ability to keep the lines of communication open.

Once a vision has been articulated and a strategy devised, the team members have to be mobilized to make it happen. It is imperative that intention be translated into action. Believing in one's dream is not sufficient; our world is full of individuals who can dream. Even the best plans are worthless unless they attract support within the team and can be fully implemented.

The Globe and Mail newspaper disclosed the results of a survey of the goals of some three hundred senior U.S. executives. More than 80 percent stated they had a clear vision of how they wanted their companies to evolve. More than 70 percent said they felt their visions could be achieved. "However, the survey also stated that the major stumbling block was not in generating the vision, rather it was in persuading others to share the vision and convert it into reality." Learning to communicate the vision is critical.

Conveying the vision may well involve different dimensions of communication. It certainly will include verbal explanations to staff and lay leaders of what the vision is, so they can imagine the potential. This needs to happen in large groups, small groups and one-on-one—building momentum requires continually keeping the vision before the people.

Another dimension of communication is non-verbal. According to studies, 55 percent of a message is communicated by body language, 38 percent by the tone of voice and approximately seven percent by actual words. The adage "you cannot not communicate" has significant implications for leaders. If leaders take a passive rather than active attitude towards the vision and the potential of people, their seeming lack of passion will be evident and will affect others on the team.

Who communicates the vision? That depends largely on who formulated it. If the team leader is the one with the vision, he becomes the primary catalyst for making it known. If others helped establish the vision, having them communicate it is an added benefit. With the young adult renewal referred to earlier, the ten who constituted our core group effectively communicated the vision with a spirit of enthusiasm that penetrated the target group and overflowed to the entire congregation.

Regardless of who the author of the vision is, a primary responsibility of the leader is to continually communicate this sense of purpose. This will develop and maintain support, energy and whole-hearted participation in the ministry.

Relational involvement

Teamwork involves more than the willingness to cooperate together on a given task. What most people appreciate in teamwork is the qualitative dimension. It is that feeling that gets expressed as "We work closely together" or "We all helped each other." Such are the experiences of people who have positive work relationships.

Perhaps the key distinction between a committee and a team is this relational component. The word team means "collections of people who must rely on group collaboration if each member is to experience the optimum success and goal achievement."[10] In a committee people band together to get a task completed with as little relational involvement as possible. Teams operate differently. They know that the glue that bonds them together is not simply the task but the relationships that team members develop.

Bill Fox, division manager for a major research company says, "The 10,000 runners in a New York City marathon race have a common goal or purpose. However, they are not a team. In fact, they are in competition with each other." On the other hand, Fox argues that a relay team is a good example of a real team. "Each member of the team shares a common goal and they must work together to achieve it. All members of an 800-meter relay team must do their part by running fast, passing the baton skillfully, and encouraging each other…success will depend upon the degree to which they behave like an effective team."[11]

Remember, positive relationships tend to lend themselves to positive results. The subject of "what it feels to belong to a team" is one that is ignored in modern literature, but it was one that Nehemiah could not ignore. As we read in chapter five, Nehemiah had to address why certain people did not feel a part of the team. He communicated with them and encouraged them to *feel* a part of the group.

Individual effort is no longer enough. Despite what one thinks of Magic Johnson's personal lifestyle, there is no denying he was one of the premier guards of the NBA. In his book *The Winner Within*, Pat Riley, one of Johnson's former coaches, tells of an incident that Johnson shared with him regarding becoming a team player:

"… Earvin told me about something that had happened when he was a little boy, playing Young League basketball in East Lansing Michigan. He'd done as he was told. Because he was so gifted, he scored most of the points every game. His team won, time after time. But when he looked around at the moment of victory, hoping someone would return that big smile of his, his teammates looked miserable. They felt like nobodies. The coach's game plan was producing wins, but it was bashing the team's feelings of success and significance.

"Earvin didn't want it to be that way. It drove a wedge between him and his friends. So he decided to change his style. Instead of scoring all the points, he would draw the defenders, then pass to whoever was open. Through his unselfishness he would enhance the skills of others. He would help them experience the same kind of kinetic, contagious joy from playing that he always felt. Then they'd be motivated to be their best. The team could experience both winning and success at the same time."[12]

A willingness to sacrifice

Team members must have a willingness to make personal sacrifices for the good of the team. In his book *Coaching for Commitment*, Kinlaw suggests that two indicators can help determine the level of commitment among team members. One is the degree to which people are focused on the goal, and the other is the degree of sacrifice that people are willing to make to reach the goal.[13] A winning attitude is evidenced in the team members' willingness to sacrifice personal gain for the good of the team. There are times when being a team member requires subordinating personal interests to group interests. Too often people like to be a part of a team as long as that team will catapult them into personal success. Such self-centeredness is counterproductive to effective teamwork.

Pat Riley is one of the most successful coaches in NBA history. He highlights one of the essential ingredients of a successful team in any venture of life when he writes: "The most difficult thing for individuals to do when they're part of the team is to sacrifice. It's so easy to become selfish in a team environment. To play for *me*. It's very vulnerable to drop your guard and say, 'This is who I am and I'm gonna open up and give myself to you.' But that's exactly what you've gotta do. Willing sacrifice is the great paradox. You must give up something in the immediate present—comfort ease, recognition, quick rewards—to attract something even better in the future: a full heart and sense that you did something which counted."[14]

I am sure that the people of Nehemiah's day knew what it was like to give up something in the immediate in order to attract something better in the future. In the case of Nehemiah and the people of Israel that "something better" was the rebuilding of the walls. They also must have experienced what it is to have a "full heart and sense that they did something which counted."

Being a team player was critical for Nehemiah and every other person who chose to rebuild the wall. The task was completed, but not without obstacles. In chapter four they had to overcome the ridicule of certain individuals who pessimistically said the task could never be completed. But as a team they shared a common vision, they agreed on how the job would be completed, they pulled together while looking out for each other's concerns, and they had the proper attitude that allowed them to make the necessary sacrifices to accomplish their task. Many of the concepts of teamwork and being a team player that Nehemiah modeled are pertinent for anyone who has to compete in the workplace in the nineties.

Action Steps

1. *Enhance your peer-relating skills.* It has been estimated that promotions are most-often based on 15 percent technical skills and 85 percent on the ability to relate to people.

2. *Analyze the teams you are presently involved with*—work, church, and community. What dynamics are they exhibiting? What dynamics are lacking?

3. *Check your attitude.* Many people say they are team players, but in reality they are team players only as long as they are the quarterback. Genuine team players are those who are willing to do "whatever it takes!"

Notes

[1] Glenn M. Parker, *Teamplayers and Teamwork.* (San Francisco: Jossey-Bass Publishers, 1990), 16.

[2] Merrill E. Douglass and Donna N. Douglass, *Time Management for Team.* (New York: AMACOM, 1992), 3.

[3] Savannah News-Press, 10 February 1990.

[4] James E. Means, *Effective Pastors for a New Century.* (Grand Rapids, Baker Book House, 1993), 199–200.

[5] Quoted in Wayne E. Baker, *Networking Smart: How to Build Relationships for Personal and Organizational Success.*

[6] Douglass and Douglass, op. cit., viii.

[7] Warren Bennis and Burt Nanus, *Leaders: Strategies for Taking Charge.* (New York: Harper & Row Publishers, 1985), 92.

[8] Robert K. Greenleaf, "The Leadership Crisis", *Humanitas* 14, no.3. (November 1978): 297–308.

[9] Bennis and Nanus, op cit., 89.

[10] Douglass and Douglass, op. cit., 13.

[11] Parker, op. cit., 16–17.

[12] Pat Riley, *The Winner Within: a Life Plan for Team Players.* (New York: Putnam Publishing Group, 1993) 36–37.

[130] Dennis C. Kinlaw, *Developing Superior Work Teams: Building Quality and the Competitive Edge.* (Lexington, Mass: Lexington Books, 1991), 117.

[14] Riley, op. cit., 15.

CHAPTER EIGHT

YOUR FAITH COMMUNITY

What Americans hunger for is not more goods or greater power,
but a manner of life, restoration of the bonds between people that we call
community, a philosophy which values the individual rather then his possessions,
a sense of belonging, of shared purpose and enterprise.

RICHARD N. GOODWIN
"THE END OF RECONSTRUCTION"

The majestic Redwood trees of Northern California are known for their tremendous size. Surprisingly, the roots of these trees do not penetrate deep into the ground. Instead, their shallow roots connect together, providing the strength, support and nourishment needed to reach great heights. In a similar way, Christians are bound together and support one another to accomplish great things. In his book *Stress and the Bottom Line,* Dr. E.M. Gherman says that supportive relationships are vital to our emotional and physical health.

> People who are functioning members of their community, who are "socially healthy," also tend to have a higher degree of psychological health and physical well-being. Those people who have developed a source of social support, who have close relationships with neighbors and fellow workers, generally deal more effectively with stressful events than those who are more socially isolated.[1]

Futurist John Naisbitt in his national bestseller *Megatrends* indicates that paralleling the advancement of technology into our society has been the increased awareness of our need for closer contact with people. Naisbitt referred to this phenomena as "high tech/high touch." People are looking to self-help groups, discovery groups, and other small group experiences as a way of meeting people outside work. In the midst of our impersonal world, people are craving community.

The results of a recent Gallup poll revealed that as many as four out of ten Americans feel lonely—frequently or occasionally. Analysis of the data led to the conclusion that Americans are among the loneliest people in the world.[2]

Isolation is far too common in our highly transient society. One of the downsides of the tremendous mobility today is the isolation from extended family. It used to be that when couples or families were facing struggles they could count on the emotional strength of other family members, but that is more difficult when you live in Colorado and other family members are scattered across New England, North Dakota and Georgia. Who do you turn to for support?

Individuals are desperate for community life. People are desirous of a network of supportive relationships. One of the primary strengths of a faith community or church is that it provides a sense of community that is unique from all other forms of community. Christianity as outlined in the New Testament incorporates a spiritual experience as well as a relational experience. It is both vertical and horizontal. In the New Testament these two concepts are intricately intertwined, but for the purposes of our discussion we will examine each aspect separately. This chapter will highlight the horizontal dimension of the Christian experience, while the next chapter will focus on the vertical dimension of our relationship with God.

Ajith Fernado, in his book *Reclaiming Friendship,* records an incident from John Wesley's early life, as told in his journal. Wesley once met a person whom he calls a "serious man." The man told him, "Sir, you wish to serve God and go to heaven? Remember that you cannot serve him alone. You must therefore find companions or make them. The Bible knows nothing of solitary religion." Wesley never forgot that wise counsel. Much later he would write, "Christianity is a social religion. To turn it into a solitary religion is indeed to destroy it."[3]

God created man for relationship, and He created Christians as a family. Families need to be together. They are healthiest when they spend time with one another. Sociologists Barna and McKay note:

> Many Christians are desperate for friendships with spiritual kinfolk...Many people interviewed in our opinion surveys indicated their willingness to sacrifice first-rate preaching and Sunday School teaching for the opportunity to develop lasting bonds with other Christians.[4]

A Place to Belong

In our fractured and anxiety-driven society, all of us crave the feeling of belonging—to feel that we are part of a group, members of a community. In the latter half of this century we have become an increasingly mobile society. "The average American moves fourteen times in his life time and every decade about half the town's population moves."[5]

In our high-tech world, people crave meaningful and supportive relationships. The recipe for success in our society requires large measures of single-minded preoccupation with our concerns, mixed with equally large measures of time and energy burned up in expanding our careers, leaving little time for relationships outside work or home. With the frenzied lifestyle of urban living, is there any doubt why so many experience isolation and loneliness?

A couple of years ago, trend watcher Faith Popcorn observed the emergence of "cocooning," a trend characterized by associating with a small group of friends, having your home as your retreat, and focusing on your family. Popcorn says that this expresses itself in people having small social enclaves. By staying at home rather than going out to dinner, or renting a video rather than going out to a movie, people are returning to the idea of the family home as the center of activity, rather than as Grand Central Station.

But "cocooning" is far from what true community is about. Community is little more than a social cliche. Traditionally people looked to the church to provide a sense of community. In many small communities the church was the center of people's social lives. It was not uncommon to have someone from your family at the church every time the doors were unlocked. A family's social calendar revolved around the church. We are finding less evidence of that today, but people's quest for community remains.

Pollster George Gallup Jr., in his *National & International Religion Report,* confirms that experiencing a sense of community is one of the things people are looking for in a church. He reports that the seven needs of the average American are as follows:

1. The need for shelter and food.

2. The need to believe life is meaningful and has a purpose (a need cited by 70 percent of the respondents, with two-thirds believing most churches and synagogues are not effective in meeting it).

3. The need for a sense of community and deeper relationships (nearly one-third of Americans say they have been lonely for a long period of time in their lives).

4. The need to be appreciated and respected (or, as one person put it, "The closer people feel to God, the better they feel about themselves").

5. The need to be listened to and heard ("Americans overwhelmingly think the future of the church will be shaped by the laity more than by the clergy...they believe it will happen, they believe it should happen").

6. The need to feel one is growing in faith.

7. The need for practical help in developing a mature faith.[6]

Our society seems to be at a loss for community. Robert Wuthnow, Director of the Study of American Religion at Princeton University, makes this commentary on our present society: "We have become a nation of individualists, obsessed with our jobs, our bank accounts, our feelings—our selves. We live in anonymous places, jealously protecting our personal privacy, and whatever hopes we entertain of finding a warm, supportive community are threatened by our incessant moving about and the pressures that impinge upon our time."[7]

A closely knit assembly appeals to our quest for community. It appeals to one of the emotional foundations of life. Everyone wants to "belong" to something. Author Saul Levine defines belonging this way:

> Belonging is our sense of community with others or our need for affiliation with others. We all want to be loved, to be understood by family and friends...We also need a wider community

of people in which we feel accepted and appreciated. Together this makes up our sense of belonging. Without it, we feel alienated from the world.[8]

Community in the New Testament

Providing a strong sense of community is one of the functions of a local church. "We were all baptized by one Spirit into one body," wrote the Apostle Paul. "If one part suffers, every part suffers with it; if one part is honored, every part rejoices with it" (1 Cor. 12:26). God designed the church to be a unique community of faith. In the New Testament the corporate aspect of our Christian experience is very pronounced. Our first glimpses of the early church are of people in community. Do you remember how the first Christian congregation was described?

All the believers were together and had everything in common. Selling their possession and goods, they gave to anyone who had need. Every day they continued to meet together in the temple courts. They broke bread in their homes and ate together with glad and sincere hearts praising God and enjoying the favor of all the people. (Acts 2:44–47a)

The word *koinonia* is used in the New Testament in reference to the special fellowship that Christians in the early church experienced. "Within the Christian tradition itself the word koinonia has always received special attention. It connotes the group of believers who constitute a community of support—support both of one another's commitments of faith and of each other's physical and emotional needs."[9]

"Evidence from recent studies indicates that for many people the church does in fact function as a community of support. Church members, particularly those who actively participate, feel they can count on one another for various kinds of help. For example, when asked, 'If you or someone in your family became seriously ill, do you think you could count on any of the following for help?', 64 percent of the public in one national survey said they would be able to count on members of a church or synagogue, and among weekly churchgoers, this proportion was 86 percent. By comparison, only 50 percent of the public thought they could count on people at work."[10] There is tremendous value in connecting with like-minded people.

A community of believers that is characterized by love, caring, and warmth is a treasure indeed.

Editor and co-founder of Youth Specialties Wayne Rice says that healthy faith communities share eight characteristics: *interaction, intensity, affirmation, corporeality, reciprocity, commitment, continuity and openness.*[11]

Interaction involves good communication. In a healthy community there are opportunities for people to get to know each other, and to dialogue with each other (see Ephesians 5: 19–20; Colossians 3:16).

Intensity measures the depth of a group's interaction. In a healthy community people are able to get below the surface and share deeply in an atmosphere of trust (Galatians 6:2; James 5:16).

Affirmation means to make positive statements to a person. In a healthy community each member is included in the group and feels appreciated by the others (1 Thessalonians 4:18; 5:11; Hebrews 3:13).

Corporeality means the group should share in ways that are practical, material or tangible. In a healthy community people share their resources with each other. They spend time together and help each other in times of trouble or need (Acts 2:44–47; Romans 12:13).

Reciprocity involves everyone in the group. In a healthy community responsibilities and benefits are shared equally among members. A healthy community is not dominated by a few members who do all the ministering, all the interacting, all the affirming, all the giving (1 Corinthians 12:7; Ephesians 4:15–16).

Commitment is required to achieve the long-term goal of becoming as one. In a healthy community, as in a marriage, commitment to each other helps keep the group together through difficult times (2 Thessalonians 2:15).

Continuity involves time—weeks, months, even years. A healthy community doesn't happen overnight; it develops slowly (Romans 15:4–5; Galatians 6:9). Time is something most of us feel in short supply of, and our culture demands everything instantly, but the community of faith will take time to develop, and will last for a long time.

Finally, *openness* invites and welcomes newcomers into the community. A healthy community is not closed or inclusive; it is not a "holy huddle," but an inviting group (Acts 2:46–47).

Your Involvement

Pollster George Barna reports, "The average adult thinks that belonging to a church is good for other people, but represents unnecessary bondage and baggage for himself."[12] People want to become involved, but perhaps they have not sensed that the church is an accepting, inviting place. Of course, having a sense of belonging does not come when people perceive the faith community as another leisure-time activity, competing with recreational activities such as a weekend at the cottage, skiing, baseball, or college classes. Belonging requires a willingness to involve oneself, not only in attending services but also in the lives of other people. Pastor R. Kent Hughes observes, "...on the most elementary level, you do not have to go to church to be a Christian. You do not have to go home to be married either. But in both cases if you do not, you will have a very poor relationship."[14]

Everyone talks about community, but few people are willing to pay the price necessary for community to be established. There is a Hasidic tale that has been told and retold that highlights the reason why community eludes us:

> A prince in a distant country dreamed of a place where people might live in perfect community—in reciprocal, fair, and loving community. The prince called together people to form such a community through a covenant together. As a sign of their covenant, the prince asked each person to bring a bottle of his or her finest wine. When they arrived at the place where the covenant was to be made, each person was to take his or her bottle of expensive wine and pour it into a great bowl to symbolize that each person was bringing his or her best gifts to form the community.

> But one man thought to himself, "If I bring my finest bottle of wine and pour it in with everyone else's wine, what good would that do? All of the distinctive bouquet, flavor, and character of my wine will be lost, swallowed up with everyone else's wine." So he decided to take a bottle of his most expensive wine, pour out the contents, and fill the bottle with water. 'Who is to know the difference? That way I will not be wasting my precious vintage."

The day for the founding of the community came and each poured the content of his or her bottle into the great bowl. Then the prince had everyone take a cup and drink from the bowl. To everyone's horror, it was water! Every single person had done what that man had done. They all substituted water for wine. Then the prince knew that he would not have his dream for community. No one there was willing to pay the price for true community.[14]

Action Steps

1. *Visit some local Bible-believing churches* in your local community if you do not presently belong to a faith community.

2. *Choose a church.*

3. *Then look for ways to get involved.* Go to the pastor and ask what needs to be done.

4. *Take the time to establish supportive relationships* with fellow Christians to strengthen your daily walk with God. A small group or an accountability partner is essential if you are going to be an integral part of the Christian community.

Notes

[1] Quoted in Rick Yohn, *Finding Time: A Christian Approach to Life Management.* (Waco, Tex.: Word Books 1984), 152.

[2] Nashville *Banner* 18 July, 1987.

[3] Ajith Fernado, *Reclaiming Friendship: Relating to Each Other in a Frenzied World.* (Scottsdale, Penn.: Herald Press, 1993), 24.

[4] George Barna and William Paul MacKay, *Vital Signs.* (Westchester, Ill.: Crossway Books, 1984), 123.

[5] Lee Strobel, *Inside the Mind of Unchurched Harry and Mary.* (Grand Rapids: Zondervan Publishing House, 1993), 61.

[6] Quoted in Leith Anderson, *A Church for the Twenty-first Century.* (Minneapolis: Bethany House Publishers, 1992), 214.

[7] Robert Wuthnow, *Christianity in the Twenty-first Century: Reflections and Challenges Ahead.* (New York: Oxford University Press, 1993), 32–33.

[8] Saul Levine, *Phoenix from the Ashes: Rebuilding Shattered Lives.* (Toronto: Key Porter Books, 1992), 3.

[9] Wuthnow, op. cit., 33.

[10] Wuthnow, op. cit., 33.

[11] Wayne Rice, "A Community-Building Church—A People Who Care", *Decision,* April 1992, 27-29.

[12] George Barna, *The Frog in a Kettle.* (Ventura, Calif.: RegalBooks, 1991), 133.

[13] R. Kent Hughes, *Disciplines of a Godly Man.* (Wheaton, Ill.: Crossway Books, 1991), 157.

[14] Thomas H. Naylor, William H. Willimon, and Magdalena R. Taylor, *The Search for Meaning.* (Nashville, Tenn.: Abingdon Press, 1994), 132.

CHAPTER NINE

YOUR SPIRITUAL DIRECTOR

If there is light in the soul, There will be beauty in the person.
If there is beauty in the person, There will be harmony in the house.
If there is harmony in the house, There will be order in the nation.
If there is order in the nation, There will be peace in the world.
ANCIENT WISDOM

One Saturday morning a minister was frantically trying to prepare his sermon under the most difficult conditions. His wife was out doing errands. It was a rainy day, and his young daughter was restless and bored, with little to do. Finally, in desperation, the minister picked up an old magazine and thumbed through it until he came to a large brightly colored picture. It showed a map of the world. He tore the page from the magazine, shredded it into little pieces and scattered the scraps all over the living room floor with the instructions, "If you can put this page together, I'll give you fifty cents."

The preacher hoped this might keep his daughter occupied for most of the morning, but within ten minutes there was a knock at his study door. His daughter had completed the puzzle. The minister was amazed to see that the girl had finished the project so soon, with the pieces of paper neatly arranged and the map of the world back in order.

"How did you get it done so fast?" the dad inquired.

"Oh, it was easy," his daughter replied. "On the other side there is a person's picture. I just put the piece of paper on the bottom under the scraps, put the picture of the person together, put a piece of paper on the top, and then turned it over. I figured that if I got the person right, the world would be right." Her father smiled, and handed her fifty cents. "Not only have you earned the fifty cents, but you've given me my sermon for tomorrow. If the person is right, his world will be right." In many respects bringing order to our relational world requires that we cultivate the relationship that impacts all others in our relational constellation—our relationship with God. In essence, it is this relationship that becomes the compass that enables us to navigate the complexities of life and to keep our relational world in balance.

Cultivating Intimacy with God

God is a relational being. He desires communion with the individuals of His creation (Rev. 3:20). As Christians we have simply responded to the invitation to dialogue with Him.

I wasted an hour one morning beside a mountain stream,
I seized a cloud from the sky above
    and fashioned myself a dream,
In the hush of early twilight, far from the haunts of men,
I wasted a summer evening and fashioned my dream again.

Wasted? Perhaps.
Folks say so who have never walked with God...
When lanes are purple with lilacs or yellow with golden rods,
But I have found strength for my labors
    in that one short evening hour.
I have found joy and contentment,
I have found peace and power.
My dreaming has left me a treasure,
A hope that is strong and true,
From wasted hours I have built my life and
Found my faith anew.

Author Unknown

In chapter six we said that a marriage is not a contract, but a relationship designed to be a vibrant and life-changing experience. For that to occur people have to nurture it. Tragically, however, men as well as women taken a similar approach in their commitment to God that they have taken in their marriages. They have acted selfishly, looking for what they can get out of the relationship, rather than committing to a person they love. Too many make a decision to accept Christ and then get on with living their lives. From their point of view, the spiritual dimension has been taken care of, so now they want to move on to something else. Such a static approach to relationships does not work in marriage, nor will it work in our Christian experience. Static Christianity occurs when a person makes a decision to become a Christian, then simply puts his spiritual life in neutral.

Authentic Christianity, on the other hand, involves much more than making a decision and then focusing exclusively on running one's life. Authentic Christianity involves developing a *relationship* with a living, speaking, dynamic and personal God. Perhaps part of the reason some people have a static Christian experience is that they have a static view of God. Static in the sense that their perception of God is that He no longer dialogues with His people. He has ceased communicating. My own Christian experience was radically transformed when I came to an understanding that God is still a living, dynamic, communicating God. He continues to be in the business of changing the lives of His people, just as He did in Bible times.

Reflecting upon my religious heritage, this was a concept foreign to me. It was not that I didn't believe that God never communicated (obviously He did so in the Bible), it was I didn't feel that He would communicate with me in a personal way. The Bible records for us the history of men encountering God in dynamic and personal ways. God was creative in His communication patterns. At times God communicated through an angel, on other occasions He gave dreams, prophecy, visions, or a word of wisdom or knowledge. The Hebrews I passage is sometimes cited as the prooftext indicating that God ceased to communicate directly with His people, "In the past God spoke to our forefathers through the prophets of many times and in various ways but in these last days he has spoken to us by His Son..." (Hebrews 1:2–3).

However, the author of the book of Hebrews is not saying that God has changed or that He has ceased to communicate, rather He has given us the supreme form of communication—His Son, Jesus. God has now added the visual to His verbal presentation. Jesus, "the exact representation of his being" has come as the ultimate but not final form of communication between God and His people.

Pastor and author Bill Hybels notes, "It makes no sense to believe that God lost His voice at the end of the first century. If the essence of Christianity is a personal relationship between the almighty God and individual beings, it stands to reason that God still speaks to believers today."[1] *God is still in the business of communicating with people today, as He was in Bible times.* Samuel 3:1–10 records the account of one young man who heard God's voice. An examination of this narrative reveals several principles that can be gleaned with respect to hearing His voice.

Remember to listen. The narrative begins with the observation, "In those days the word of the Lord was rare, there were not many visions" (vs. 1). The first principle that can be gleaned is that God's still, small voice is not heard when His people are not listening.

One may ask whether it was a matter of people not listening or God not speaking, but author Stanley Jones notes, "Actually one follows the other. When God's people ignore God's leading, God stops speaking."

An expression that is applicable to many aspects of life is "use it or lose it." If you choose not to exercise your old high school Spanish, you will lose your ability to speak it. In the same way, if you choose to ignore the Lord and His Word, you will lose the ability to hear Him. Dag Hammarskjold, former United States Ambassador to the United Nations, once wrote, "How can you keep your powers of hearing when you never want to listen?"

In the play "Saint Joan," by George Bernard Shaw, Joan of Arc is always hearing voices from God, and this angers the king. He complains to her, "Oh, your voices! Your voices! Why don't your voices come to me? I'm the king not you!" Joan's plaintive answer is, "They do come, but you do not hear them. You're not out in the field in the evening listening for them."

Time is a valuable commodity for many today. Time is quickly becoming the "new currency we utilize for determining what is of value to us," says Christian futurist George Barna.[2] The problem is that people are not scheduling times of stillness that makes such communication possible.

God does not shout, He whispers. God chose to speak in the quietness of the evening when Eli and Samuel were getting ready to retire.

"And it happened at that time as Eli was lying down in his place (now his eyesight had begun to grow dim and he could not see well), and the lamp of the God had not gone out, and Samuel was lying down in the temple of the Lord where the ark of God was, that the Lord called Samuel" (v. 2–4a). Gordon MacDonald, in his book *Ordering Your Private World,* discusses the necessity of being still before God in silence. He quotes Mother Teresa as saying, "We need to find God, and He cannot be found in noise and restlessness. God is the friend of silence." Mother Teresa goes on to discuss the value of such silence to one's engagement in ministry with people:

> "...The more we receive in silent prayer, the more we can give in our active life. We need silence to be able to touch souls. The essential thing is not what we say, but what God says to us and through us."[3]

When I pastored I often wondered as I examined the lifestyle of my leaders, "Where does the still small voice of God get heard?" Too often our lives are filled with endless activities. It should come as no surprise that the experience of hearing God's voice is rare. If we are going to have such experiences, we have to take the time and learn the discipline of coming before God in silence, listening for His voice.

Invite God to speak. A third aspect of Samuel's encounter with God involves inviting God to speak to us. Young Samuel, confused as to the source of the voice he hears, goes to Eli for clarification. The aging priest, though not a Godly man, has the wherewithal to realize that it is God calling the boy. Eli then directs Samuel to respond to the voice of God and invite Him to speak. Upon hearing the voice for a third time Samuel says, "Speak, Lord, for your servant is listening" (vs. 10).

Once we realize that God does desire to communicate, and come before Him in stillness and silence, it is appropriate to invite Him to speak. Bill Hybels provides some windows into his listening exercises in his book, *Honest to God?.* As part of his daily time spent with God, Hybels takes the time to listen to the Lord. He begins with a simple prayer: "Lord, you tallked to your children all through history and you said that You're an unchangeable God. Talk to me now. I'm listening. I'm open."[4]

Hybels follows that by asking four questions: *What is the next step in my relationship with You? What is the next step in the development of my character? What is the next step in my family life? And what is the next step in my ministry?* You may have different questions, but the important thing is that you create an opportunity for God to dialogue back to you. One need not expect the answers to come in the form of an audible voice. For many people, God speaks through an impression or persistent thought.

Be willing to respond. A fourth and final principle is that we need to be willing to listen and be obedient. For young Samuel his obedience was marked by a life of service to God. You see, tuning in to God's voice is not intended to be a personal, meditative trip. It can be one of the ways God provides guidance and direction for our lives. More often than not, such prompting demands courage to seek or extend forgiveness. Courage to share one's faith with a friend that God has placed upon your heart. Courage to follow God in a ministry opportunity. If we continually choose to ignore the voice of God, it should come as no surprise that we are no longer tuned into His voice.

The resistance by some to listen to God is perhaps because of the abuses we have seen by those who claim to be listening to God. Cult leaders who have led followers into all sorts of evil claim, "God led me to do this." We evangelicals have become afraid of the concept of God communicating directly with us—even though that is how God has communicated with His people throughout the ages.

One rule of thumb to follow in this matter of listening to His voice is to remember that all messages coming from God will be consistent with His Word. God will never guide a person to something that is contrary to His general will as revealed in Scripture. Joyce Huggett adds a further guideline when she says the issue is "not newness but nowness."[5] It is an important distinction to be made. We are not in search of further revelation of God. We are wanting to be in contact with what God wants to do in our lives now. It is this "nowness" that can transform our Christian existence from that of a static experience to an authentic and intimate one with God the Father, through His Son, Jesus Christ. "Jesus Christ is alive and here to teach His people himself," writes Richard Foster. 'is voice is not hard to hear, his vocabulary is not hard to understand, but we must learn to hear his voice and obey it."

I am convinced that if we hold strongly to the conviction that God is a living, dynamic, communicating God, it will significantly alter the way we approach Him and radically transform a static Christian decision into a vibrant and authentic experience.

The Assistance of a Spiritual Director

While our relationship with Jesus Christ is a personal one, it can be aided by the assistance of another human being. Samuel was confused as to what was going on. When Eli, someone with more experience in these matters, instructed him on an appropriate response, Samuel was able to discern and understand God's voice.

There can be times in our spiritual experience when the assistance of a more mature brother or sister in Christ can enable us to more accurately discern God's voice and God's leading in our lives. Throughout the history of Christianity, men and women who had wrestled with issues pertaining to the soul have sought and received spiritual direction. "A closer look at the lives of holy men and women throughout the history of Christianity shows us that those who searched with great fervor for an intimate relationship with God always asked for guidance and direction."[6]

One also has to put history in its context. Christians of former centuries did not have access to the large volumes of written material, radio, or television teaching that we have today. They were much more dependent on interpersonal exchanges to glean from each other's insights regarding spiritual development.

The question, "What is a spiritual director?" may best be answered by identifying what spiritual direction is not.

First, spiritual direction is not naval gazing. Spiritual direction challenges us to look within ourselves and to examine the interior dimensions of our lives, for a purpose. As the philosopher once noted, "The unexamined life is not worth living." It is in our best interests to periodically assess the direction of our lives. Is God calling us to something new? Are there some changes that need to be made? By nature most of us are not introspective people. At the same time we live at a pace of life that does not lend itself to much thinking.

Second, spiritual direction is not discipleship. In evangelical circles we talk a great deal about discipleship. But spiritual direction is not discipleship. Discipleship is generally referred to as the process of helping a Christian get rooted and grounded in Christ and His Word. Both are indispensable for a Christian, particularly a new believer.

Discipleship is often top-down. Someone, usually the discipler, takes the initiative to teach another person the essential truths of the faith. Spiritual direction is distinct from this process in several ways. One is that spiritual direction is initiated by the person seeking assistance, not by the spiritual director. Another is that spiritual direction is not a prepackaged program that one enrolls in for six weeks or thirteen weeks or even two years. Spiritual direction is likely to be a short term relationship, with no pre-set curriculum. Finally, spiritual direction is distinct from discipleship in that it is primarily a *reflective* process rather than an *instructional* process.

Third, spiritual direction is not vocational mentoring. Career or ministry decisions are not the only questions that individuals ponder. There are other questions that people wrestle with from time to time, questions that are not of financial or medical or legal matters. They are questions that pertain to the soul, to matters of the heart.

What then is spiritual direction?

Spiritual direction may be formal or informal. An informal relationship meets regularly for an extended period of time; two friends dialoguing about the truths of God's Word, discerning God's leading in their lives. They hold each other accountable for spiritual disciplines. Sometimes two people will agree to read a chapter from the same book and periodically meet to discuss it. This kind of arrangement is often referred to as a *soul friend.*

1. A more formal relationship may occur when you mutually agree to meet regularly for six to eight months and discuss matters pertaining to the soul. It may take the form of a spiritual audit. Stanley and Clinton provide a checklist to gauge one's need for a spiritual director:

2. It is always wise to have a "spiritual checkup," just as from time to time you need a physical checkup.

3. When you sense you've reached a plateau in personal, spiritual, or ministry growth, you may be facing an obstacle to growth, and you may need the perspective and insight of a Spiritual Guide.

4. When you find that you repeatedly ask questions about growth, or you are being challenged from more than one source for growth, then you probably need a Spiritual Guide. Frequently, others can sense your lack of growth before you can.

5. If you experience a need for an attitude change or you begin to experience spiritual struggles, you probably need the help of a Spiritual Guide.

6. If you are in a place of spiritual influence or authority and have no intimate accountability with someone or some group of spiritually mature people, then you need a Spiritual Guide. Senior pastors, gifted leaders of denominations or para-church organizations, and upper-level Christian leaders frequently find that they have little spiritual accountability. Many have fallen for just such a lack of intimate accountability. [7]

Precedents of Spiritual Direction in Scripture

The truest model of spiritual direction is found in the ministry of Jesus Christ. There are several instances of people seeking an audience with Jesus to discuss matters pertaining to the soul. Nicodemus in John's Gospel came to Jesus at night to discover spiritual matters on a one-to one basis. Nicodemus was a seeker, someone in pursuit of the truth. He acknowledged that Jesus is a "Rabbi," a guide in helping people understand God and His ways in the world. That is exactly what Jesus did. He answered Nicodemus' questions.

Another example of Jesus as spiritual director is found in the exchange of the rich young ruler (Luke 18:18-29). He comes to Jesus with a spiritual question, and Christ gives him a spiritual answer. Much of being involved in the spiritual direction process is vocalizing our thoughts or struggles with someone who is further down the path. In this case the man wanted to know the pathway to eternal life. Jesus outlined the biblical teaching, and the young ruler assured Jesus that he had fulfilled scripture. Jesus, recognizing there was a major impediment to this man's walk with God, challenged him to put his security in God and not in his accumulated wealth. It was guidance the young man refused.

Sometimes a spiritual director, if he or she has the courage, may challenge us to be more honest with ourselves. Our initial reaction may be, "Who do you think you are?" But if we perceive this person has our best interests at heart, we can be thankful for their input and learn from them.

I recognize that spiritual direction has become popularized in the last decade. The interest is coming because people have a vacuum in their spiritual lives. They attend church but find it a whirl-wind of religious activity, the place of perpetual programming and how-to sermonettes. There is very little room for evaluating our spiritual progress or for personalized, pro-active spiritual care.

A glance at a Christian bookstore gives evidence that spiritual direction is as needed as ever. Unfortunately, books are no substitute for the relational element that is a part of spiritual direction. Is there anything more spiritual about reading a book written by Charles Swindoll than talking with a godly member of your church as you struggle in your experience of Christianity? Of course not. Too few Christians have developed a personal relationship with someone in their local church.

You might be wondering "Isn't that what pastors are supposed to be doing?" The answer is, of course, "Yes," but unfortunately the present paradigms of pastoral ministry are such that pastors find their time consumed with "running the church," and there is very little time remaining to assist individuals in the expansion of their souls. Having been in pastoral ministry for ten years, I am acutely aware of the pressures and expectations of pastoral ministry in the North American Christian culture. Many pastors are more "church manager" than "spiritual guide," because that is what their congregations expect of them.

"But," you ask, "Isn't that what the Word of God and the work of the Holy Spirit are to do? Why cultivate such a relationship if I already have at my disposal all the resources I need?" A spiritual director is not in competition with these resources but, as many saints before us have learned, a spiritually sensitive person can work in cooperation with the Word and the Spirit to provide guidance and direction.

The blame for lack of interest does not lie at the doorsteps of the church or on the pastor's shoulders. Christians themselves have to take responsibility for their spiritual growth. The biggest misunderstanding by evangelical Christians in the process of spiritual direction has often been that "our relationship with God is so personal, so private, so intimate, and so unique, that it cannot be the subject of guidance, and certainly not of direction."[8] We engage in what has been called "do-it-yourself Christianity." Christ never intended the personal transformation to be an isolated experience. We need to learn how to be inter-dependent, how to trust others and rely on others.

The National Football league suspended Lawrence Taylor, the New Giants perennial All Pro linebacker, for violating its substance-abuse policy. He was quoted, in the September 1, 1988, *New York Times*, saying, "God, I didn't mean for it to happen. I wish it hadn't, but I made a bad decision and I'll have to pay the price for it...I really wasn't allowing the Giants to help me. I wasn't allowing my wife to help me. I was doing it by myself and trying to make it happen by myself because *I wanted to say I could do it on my own*. It doesn't work like that. Boy, I found that out."[9]

I think pastors themselves need to seek a spiritual director, preferably not someone in their congregation. Pastors, like anyone else, are prone to disclose only what places them in a good light. In addition to maintaining their professional image, pastors also think that their pastoral preparation has given them everything they need for a lifetime of pastoral ministry. Many think they are "thoroughly equipped for every good work." The late Bill Leslie, pastor of LaSalle Street Church in downtown Chicago for many years, was once asked, "How do you recover from your emotional exhaustion?" In response he shared an episode from his own experience:

"When there was all that conflict over our building program[7] I finally said, 'I'm at the bottom; I need something!' There's a Catholic retreat center the church had used because it was close by (and when I came to LaSalle, there were only two people in the church with cars). Going there, I heard good things about a nun named Ann Wilder who did a lot of counseling. I make a to-do list every week, and every week for two years I'd written 'contact Ann Wilder' on my list. When I finally hit bottom, I did.

"I told her my situation, and she said, 'Bill, I want you to come up with a word that characterizes how you feel right now. In fact, I want the first word that comes to your mind.'

"I said, 'I feel raped.'

" 'Who raped you?'

"I said, 'I know theologically that God doesn't rape anybody, but I feel raped by God. I want to leave the church, but I knew I wouldn't be in God's will anywhere else. My wife wants to leave. I feel caught between God and Adrienne.

" 'I also feel God hasn't prepared me. In the city especially you have to learn how to exegete your neighborhood and your church as well as the Bible, and I hadn't been trained to do that. Everything is trial and error, and we've made a lot of dumb mistakes, used and maybe abused a lot of people. I feel God isn't giving us enough money or leaders... to do what He's called us to do.'

"She said, 'Who else has raped you?'

"I said, 'The church. Everybody comes to me for something, but no one takes care of me. I can ask for anything for somebody else, but I never can ask for anything for myself. I can't say, 'I need this." I feel like an orange; the church has squeezed every bit of juice out of me. '

"She said, 'Anybody else?'

"I said, 'Yeah, the community has raped me. Everybody depends on my networks. Just about any organization in the community that wants money or something asks me to write the proposals.'

"Finally she wisely said (and I've learned to do this with others), 'Would you mind if I change your image? Let's change the image from that of rape to that of a farm pump. Let's say that everybody who comes by grasped the handle and pumps.'

" 'They sure do.'

"So Anne said to me, 'Have you read those passages in the Bible on servanthood?'

" 'Yes. Those passages are the ones that got me in this trouble.'

" 'Do you believe them?' she asked.

" 'Yeah,' I said, 'I believe them, but it doesn't feel good.'

"And she said, 'The real problem is your pipe isn't deep enough. You're pumping surface water, so by 10:30 in the morning they've pumped you dry. Deep down there are underground streams. If you can get your pipe down there, there's so much water that no matter how much anybody pumps out of you, they'll have a hard time lowering that one inch. That water is always cool. Even though the pump is used a lot, the water goes up through the pump, and the pump is refreshed. Have you ever heard that passage in John 7, "Out of the innermost being shall flow rivers of living water"? That's what I'm talking about.'

"She winked a little and added, 'I guess what I'm telling you, Bill, is that you need a personal relationship with Jesus Christ.'

"I said, 'Where I went to school, I'm supposed to be saying that to you.' She knew I had one, but she was trying to say, 'Way down deep...you're shallow.' But I didn't know anybody who had anything deeper than I did.

"She said, 'If you're serious about this and will commit yourself to coming one day a month, I will serve as your spiritual director, and I think I can help you get that pipe down deep where the people can pump you, but you will stay refreshed. You'll get tired every now and then, but you'll be refreshed and energized.'

"So I worked with her and had some profound inner experiences. I go to the center now twice a month, all day. I've found as I've gotten older that I have to take in as well as give out. If there's anything a servant character has a hard time doing, it's taking care of yourself."[10]

Action Steps

Every person at some point in their lives has to make a personal decision, either to embrace God or reject Him. If you choose to embrace God you begin a pilgrimage of growing in your knowledge of Him through a personal relationship. While that relationship is intensely personal (no one else can make the decision for you) many Christians have experienced the benefit of being aided through the guidance and direction of a spiritual director.

1. *Pray* for God's leading with respect to an individual who may serve as a spiritual director in your life.

2. *Approach someone* in your church to be your spiritual director. What qualities should you keep in mind? Let me suggest four. First, pick someone who is possessed by the Spirit—someone who has an authentic and consistent walk with God. Second, choose someone with a high level of spiritual maturity. Implied in this is the fact that this person has experience in matters of the soul. Next, select someone who is learned. This does not refer exclusively to formal education nor does it negate it. I recommend people who are committed to continual learning in matters related to spiritual growth and Bible knowledge. Finally, pick someone who demonstrates the gift of discernment.

3. *Be accountable to someone.* Due in large part to the scandals that have brought the integrity of high-profile Christian leaders into

question, the issue of accountability is again gaining popularity. In *Dropping Your Guard,* Charles Swindoll defines accountability as:

- being willing to explain one's actions;

- being open, unguarded, and non-defensive about one's motives;

- answering for one's life;

- supplying the reason why.[11]

Accountability is not just for religious leaders. It is a key to maturity and character growth in the life of every Christian.

Notes

[1] Bill Hybels, *Too Busy Not to Pray.* (Downers Grove, Ill: InterVarsity Press, 1986), 109.

[2] George Barna, *The Frog in the Kettle.* (Ventura, Calif.: RegalBooks, 1991).

[3] Gordon MacDonald, *Ordering Your Private World.* (Nashville, Tenn.: Oliver-Nelson Books, 1985), 126–27.

[4] Bill Hybels, *Honest to God?* (Grand Rapids: Zondervan Publishing House, 1990), 25.

[5] Joyce Huggett, *The Joy of Listening to God.* (Downers Grove, Ill., InterVarsity Press, 1986).

[6] Henri Nouwen in Kenneth Leech, *Soul Friend: the Practice of Christian Spirituality.* (San Francisco: Harper and Row Publishers, 1977), vii.

[7] Paul D. Stanley and J. Robert Clinton, *Connecting.* (Colorado Springs: NavPress, 1992), 60–69.

[8] Nouwen in Leech op. cit., vi.

[9] Quoted in Patrick M. Morley, *The Man in the Mirror.* (Brentwood, Tenn.: Wolgemuth Hyatt Publishers, Inc., 1989), 283.

[10] "Interview with Bill Leslie", *Leadership,* Summer 1988: 16–17.

[11] Charles R Swindoll, *Dropping Your Guard.* (Waco, Tex.: Word Books, 1983) 171

CHAPTER TEN

TOXIC RELATIONSHIPS

God grant me serenity to accept the things I cannot change,
courage to change the things I can, and wisdom to know the difference.
ATTRIBUTED TO FRIEDRICH OETINGER
(1702–1782)

During the past several years we have witnessed the tragic devastation of our global community. Accidents involving toxic materials—from the leakage of carbon monoxide in India to the chemical reaction in the Ukraine—have severely damaged our environment. We are becoming acutely aware of the devastation these toxic chemicals can have if they are not handled properly.

Dr. Walter Staples has noted, "We have progressed very far in devising and developing incredible technologies to manage and control our physical environment. Yet we have not progressed nearly as far in dealing with our human environment—other people."[1]

Having mutually enhancing relationships is a tremendous and invaluable asset. We are well aware of the impact of relationships on shaping character, values, and beliefs, as well as the ability to influence the quality of our lives. The people we associate with play a powerful role in shaping our character, enhancing our effectiveness, and contributing to our happiness.

However, people are like a double-edged sword. On the one hand they can be our greatest source of pleasure. Whenever social scientists seek to discover the sources of inner happiness, participants consistently suggest that friends are one of the highest, if not *the* highest, sources of enjoyment in life. At the same time most agree that relationships can be a source of tremendous stress. Linus in the *Peanuts* cartoon once said, "I love mankind—it's people I can't stand!" I'm sure you know that feeling of loving people, yet finding them to be responsible for your greatest sorrows. As the caption on one poster stated: "It's hard to soar with the eagles when you have to live with the turkeys."

One of the pioneers of modern psychology, Sigmund Freud, observed that most of the frustrations we face in life fall under three main categories: the physical world (your car won't start on the way to work); our own limitations (you can't remember the answer to the question your boss is asking) and other people. For many of us, our greatest irritation in life comes from people—a boss, a co-worker, a mother-in-law, or perhaps another family member. Many must deal with conflict, criticism, and competitiveness on a regular basis. We all have at least one difficult person in our lives. Few of us go through life without having some difficult relational challenges along the way.

Former Denver Broncos coach John Ralston explained his departure from the team this way: 'I left because of illness and fatigue. The fans were sick and tired of me."

While visiting one of my parishioners one day, I came across a welcome mat with the inscription: "Some people bring joy wherever they go, others bring joy when they go." People are our greatest source of joy and our greatest source of frustration.

Most of us are familiar with the distinction VIP—very important people. Author Gordon MacDonald claims there are also VDP's—"Very Draining People." They are people who affect our spiritual passion and our vitality. They do so by draining it, and they do so relentlessly. MacDonald adds, 'I know that some will quickly wish to argue that there is a certain kind of energy that develops merely from the joy of serving the hurting and the lonely, and I would not want to argue with that. What I want to point out, however, is that sort of joy lasts only so long and then, in most cases, changes to a kind of exhaustion that must be addressed quickly or it will have ill effects."[2]

I have learned that draining people cost energy and passion, and that effective people who permit an imbalance of contact with these people can expect to pay a massive bill of inner exhaustion. You and I need to be aware of the effect that difficult people have on us.

Toxins Come in Different Forms

Just as there are various kinds of poisons, you'll find toxic personalties come in a variety of forms. Each one is difficult in some unique way. To be honest, we are all difficult at various times, and perhaps every person can be hard to get along with at one time or another. But some people are difficult in a chronic fashion. The toxic fumes of such relationships may come in various forms: *negativism, criticisms, or competitiveness.*

Negaholics

Nehemiah, in seeking to encourage the people of Israel to rebuild the wall of Jerusalem, encountered some discouraging situations, some of which were toxins in the form of people. In chapter four we find Nehemiah, who is attempting to do something positive for God, encountering someone determined to be negative—Sanballat. "When Sanballat heard that we were rebuilding the wall, he became angry and mocked the Jews."

I had one man on my church board who voted "no" to every proposal for change that the pastoral leadership team put forward—a true naysayer. Dealing with him was difficult and reminded me of the story of a hunter who had two incredibly negative friends. One day that hunter bought a very unusual dog—a dog that could walk on water. He took his two hunting buddies and headed off to the swamp to do some duck hunting. Whenever the hunters shot down a duck, the dog would run across the top of the water and retrieve the dead animal. The hunter waited for his partners to comment on the dog's unusual ability. Each time the other two said nothing. After the third time, the hunter in frustration blurted out, "Don't you guys notice something unusual about my dog?"

"Yes," they both replied. "Your dog can't swim."

Negative thinking is an inescapable cancer of society. It has always been here. It will always be here. Even people of high standing are plagued with this disease. In 1899, Charles Duell, commissioner of the United States Patent Office, urged President McKinley to abolish the patent office. His reason? He was convinced that everything that could be invented had been invented."[5] Stay away from "negaholics." Their negativity will darken your day.

Criticism

Criticism was one of those things I always felt was better to give than to receive. As Charles Swindoll observed in his book, *Hand Me Another Brick*, 'You cannot constantly hear criticism and negativism without having some of it rub off on you. If you are prone to discouragement, you can't run the risk of spending a lot of your time with people who traffic in discouraging and critical information."[5] If we let negative emotions fester within us, like a cancer, we are worse off as a result. Harriet Braiker, author of Lethal Lovers and Poisonous People, says:

> Technically, another person's actions do not directly damage your physical health, except in obvious cases where there is a literal infliction of bodily harm. But what quite literally can kill you—or certainly make you vulnerable to a host of health problems—is your negative reaction to your perception of the relationship. Phenomena once believed to be purely psychological—thinking, feeling, or acting—now are known to be connected to actual physiological events in the body. Relationships, then, can become toxic by creation patterns of thought or behavior that produce potent psychological poisons.[6]

One summer I had a job that forced me to work alongside a married couple. It was one of those relationships where the chemistry just was not pleasant. The discomfort started early in our working relationship when they perceived their role to be my supervisor, but I perceived our roles as being on the same level, reporting to the same administrator. Throughout the summer, whenever something did not go well with my youth program (Murphy developed his now famous law while working with youth groups), they made a special point to highlight all shortcomings with respect to my area of responsibility. If they heard any criticisms from any of the guests at the camp, they made a point of repeating them for my benefit. It is hard to remain positive in a critical environment.

Criticism is like corrosion—stay away from it and keep yourself strong and clean.

Competitiveness

Competitiveness is not limited to the athletic arena. Sometimes competition brings out the best in us, other times the worst. We find competitiveness in corporate offices as people jockey for promotions, in the political arena between rivals, and in churches where pastors compare bodies, buildings and bucks.

There was a time in King Saul's life in which he felt threatened by a young up-and-comer in his army, named David. After one of David's triumphant battles the chant "Saul has slain his thousands, and David his tens of thousands" was being shouted in the streets. Naturally Saul did not appreciate what he heard. David was not consciously competing with Saul, but the King was feeling threatened at the prospect of losing his popularity to the young hero. Envy began to grip Saul's heart, and on one occasion the hatred was so strong that Saul actually flung a spear at young David (1 Sam. 9–10). Competitiveness can become unhealthy if you resort to tearing the other person down or compete just to flaunt your pride.

Difficult relationships develop for any number of reasons. Negativism, criticism and competitiveness represent only three. When we are involved in these kinds of negative relationships they can have a profound effect on our lives. The fact is, toxic relationships drain you, emotionally and spiritually. Toxic relationships can cause high levels of stress, discomfort, tension, aggravation, and unhappiness. Whenever possible, attempts should be made to detoxify the relationship.

What do you do when you find yourself in a relationship that has chronic, harmful effect on your attitude, you effectiveness, your happiness, and your spiritual vitality?

Coping Strategies for Dealing with Toxic Relationships

As one person has observed, frogs have a tremendous advantage over humans—they can eat anything that bugs them. Wouldn't it be great if we could consume our relational problems rather than letting them consume us!

One of the questions we have to ask ourselves is, "Can you be a positive influence on the other person, or will you be dragged down?" Those who have had the experience of attempting to rescue someone who is drowning is well aware of the potential pitfalls of being dragged under by a frantic and panicking swimmer. Being trained to rescue a drowning individual is similar to having strategy for coping with poisonous people.

In Romans 12 Paul provides us with general principles for relating to people: "If possible, so far as it depends on you, be at peace with all men" (Rom. 12:18). I would like to paraphrase that verse: Do the best you can to get along with everyone. Yet realize that once in a while you are going to have a relationship with a difficult person that may fall short of the ideal.

A number of books outlining relational strategies for coping with toxic relationships attempt to help the reader understand the negative person—highlighting why they do what they do. Unfortunately no two people are alike and it is impossible to understand everyone's behavior. A more practical approach is to focus on our own response to difficult individuals. There is no overall strategy for coping with toxic relationships that can apply to every individual in all situations, but Paul's general instruction in Romans 12:18 can be broken down into several helpful concepts.

Recognize that you are unable to change another person. The only person you can change is you. Our initial coping response it to hope the other person will change. You cannot control the actions of another person, but you can choose your response in any situation. As author Marilyn Ferguson notes, "no one can persuade another to change. Each of us guards a gate of change that can only be opened from the inside. We cannot open the gate of another, either by argument or by emotional appeal,"[7]

Our natural response to someone's imperfection is to take that person on as a project. We can see so clearly the speck in our brother's eye and feel it is our God-given duty to remove it. Sadly, one false ideal gives birth to another. Our need for perfect people leads to a need to change people.

That expectation that we can change others sends many of us into misery. We spend much of our lives in frustration because these imperfect people around us seem impervious to our agenda for their lives. They are totally blind to our astonishing wisdom and stay stuck in their flaws.

I heard the story recently of a gardener who took great pride in his lawn. He kept it beautiful throughout the seasons. One spring his lawn was besieged with dandelions. He tried everything and still could not get rid of them. Finally he wrote the Department of Agriculture, explaining all the different dandelion deterrents he had tried and asking what he should do next. The answer came back, "Try getting used to them." That's not what he wanted to hear. That isn't what we want to hear either, but sometimes it is the best advice we can get.[8]

Anyone who has read the Bible knows that we are to be creative agents of change in the world. We are to be salt, light, ambassadors, reconcilers, and witnesses. God has given us a mandate to make a positive difference in society, and we cannot take that mandate lightly.

That does not mean, however, that we can change anybody. At best, we might be able to help someone who already wants to change. The motivation for personal transformation, though, is always internal.

The dark side of the interaction is the frustration we feel when we see what others put themselves through. It is not fun to watch people, especially people we love, wallow in self-induced agony. We feel a great need to do something, to effect change whether they want it or not. Is there anything more exasperating than seeing a vision of promise for someone who cannot see it for themselves? If an individual does not want to listen to your wisdom, there's no sense sharing it. You cannot change others, you will only do harm to your relationship.

Running away is not always a solution. The most common coping strategy for dealing with toxic relationships is to avoid the relationship altogether. You know, our way of dealing with toxic material is to minimize our exposure to it. Dr. Hans Seyle, one of the pioneers in stress management, offers a simple solution as a coping strategy for toxic relationships: Cut the toxic person out of your life. Isolate yourself from those who bring you down. While this strategy contains a certain appeal, few of us can simply cut people out of our lives, particularly if that person is a family member, a relative, or an employer.

When Dr. David Cowe was a young pastor, he was leading a church in Los Angeles that was growing rapidly and doing well. However, on the governing board he had a man who was both a negative thinker and a very cantankerous critic. Finally the situation got so bad that David resigned and took a new pastorate in Kansas City. "But," he lamented, "the week I arrived at my new church I went to the board meeting to meet the new leaders, and there sitting at the conference table, was the same guy!"[9]

It is often said that pastors don't *go* to a new church as much as they leave their old church. Unfortunately one finds himself trading one set of problems for a new set. But if avoidance is not an option, how can you help others who have attitude problems? You can at least work to limit your contact with their negativity, or you can attempt to let your positive attitude rub off on them. "There is a difference between helping those with perpetual attitude problems and enlisting them as our close friends. The closer our relationship, the more influential the attitudes and philosophies of our friends become to us. How about people who can drag us down? How can we help people who have attitude problems if we ignore them?"[10]

I believe Steve Diggs summarizes the principle best when he writes, "In order to succeed, we must deal with other people. We have to be involved in their lives. We have to respond to their needs and concerns. But we must never allow other people to direct and determine our attitudes. The goal: to be insulated from their pessimism and negativism but not isolated from them as people."[11]

Check your attitudes. Has bitterness and resentment towards someone taken root in your soul? When you begin harboring bitterness in your soul it is like a VCR in your mind that keeps playing back all those tapes of how you were victimized. Every time you resent someone, it is like taking out the movie of your pain and playing it again. Do you want that person to have that much influence on your life? Forgive those who hurt you! Instead of rehearsing that hurt over, and over, release it.

The book of Genesis tells the story of Joseph, who found himself in what we would label today as a dysfunctional home. His brothers hated him so much that they sold him for a few shekels of silver, thinking they would never see him again. By divine providence God reunited Joseph with his brothers. One would expect that Joseph would harbor bitterness and resentment for the cruel treatment he had suffered at the hands of his siblings. Bitterness has a way of eating through to the core of our hearts. But Joseph adopted a different perspective. In Genesis 50:20 we read, "You intended to harm me, but God intended it for good to accomplish what is now being done, the saving of many lives." Without denying the reality of the pain his brothers had inflicted, Joseph chose not to dwell on the injustices but to view the circumstances from a divine perspective. No matter what people have done to you, you make the choice of how to respond. Charles Swindoll wrote, "Life is ten percent what happens to you, and ninety percent how you respond to it."

Dr. Victor Frankl was a prisoner of war, witnessing the horrors of the Holocaust. At one point during the humiliating ordeal at the camp, Frankl was led into the Gestapo detention room. His captors had taken away his home and family, his cherished freedom, his possessions, even his watch and wedding ring. They had shaved his head and stripped his clothes off his body. There he stood before the German high command, under the glaring lights, being interrogated and falsely accused. He was destitute, a helpless pawn in the hands of brutal, prejudiced, sadistic men. He had nothing. No, that wasn't true. He suddenly realized there was one thing no one could ever take from him—his freedom to choose his own attitude. "No matter what anyone would ever do to him, regardless of what the future held for him, the attitude choice was his to make. Bitterness or forgiveness. To give up or to go on. Hatred or hope. Determination to endure or the paralysis of self-pity."[12]

Balance your relational network with people who make a positive contribution to your life.

In every ministry situation that we have served, my wife has had one or two people that are "relational leeches." They are people who take and take from a relationship, but they never give back. After an extended period of exposure to draining relationships, one begins to wilt.

One of the ways we can dilute the harmful exposure of too many draining relationships is to maintain a healthy balance of relationships that encourage and revitalize us. Make certain that you have adequate times of refilling your own emotional tanks.

Jesus, after ministering to a number of draining situations, withdrew to places of relational isolation for periods of time to regain his spiritual and emotional strength. We need to follow the same pattern. We are not to simply avoid every difficult person that we meet. In many cases these people provide us an opportunity for ministry. Learn to balance your life with those who need care and those who offer it.

Take responsibility for your own actions. The key to successful relationships really gets down to responsibility. You are responsible for how you treat others. You may not be responsible for how they treat you, but you are responsible for your reactions to those who are difficult. You can't choose how others will treat you, but you can choose how you will respond to them.

Hugh Sidney, a syndicated columnist for *Time,* was walking in New York City one evening with a friend who stopped to buy a newspaper. The newspaper boy was gruff and discourteous as he made change, but Harris's friend politely smiled and wished the man a nice weekend.

"A sullen fellow, isn't he?"Harris asked as the two walked on down the street.

"Oh, he's that way every night," shrugged the friend.

"Then why do you continue to be so kind to him?" Harris asked.

"Why not?" his friend responded. "Why should I let him decide how I'm going to act?"

Remember, you choose how you are going to react to negative people in your relational world. The effect of difficult relationships—whether they make us or break us—is not determined by the treatment we receive but how we respond to it.[13]

When the Toxic Fumes Overwhelm You

Not all relationships can or should be maintained. Even Paul taught that there may be relationships in which it is not possible to live in peace with all men (Rom. 16:3). "If you find relationships that are not mutually constructive, if someone brings you down rather than challenges and elevates you, then you must make a decision. Can you transform this into a healthy relationship or do you need to sever it?"[14] There may be situations where removing or distancing yourself from certain relationships may be your only viable option.

To protect your health, it may be necessary to achieve a greater degree of psychological distance from your toxic relative. Psychological distance refers to less intimacy and lower interdependence. You will need to reduce the amount of information about yourself, particularly of an intimate or personal nature, that you disclose to the relative in question. If you still crave a withholding parent's approval, you must learn to rely on your own sense of self-affirmation and the feedback of other people with whom you have healthier relationships.[15]

In David's situation with King Saul, David knew that staying in that circumstance was not an option. His physical and psychological safety were at risk. With the help of Saul's own son, Jonathan, David distanced himself by running away for a period of time. Instead of being overwhelmed by the poisonous relationship he had with a jealous king, David chose to remove himself physically. You may not have the option of removing yourself physically or geographically from a toxic relationship, but you can begin to distance yourself emotionally and socially from its exposure.

Action Steps

1. Complete a relational audit. In examining your relational network, what relationships are experiencing conflict? What relationships do you perceive have a harmful effect on you emotionally or spiritually?

2. Make each toxic relationship a matter of prayer. I've seen plaques in people's homes that say, "Prayer changes things." That is only partly true. The primary thing that prayer does is that it changes people—most often the person doing the praying. Keep in mind the serenity prayer, "God grant me serenity to accept the things I cannot change, the courage to change the things I can, and the wisdom to know the difference."

Notes

[1] Walter D. Staples, *Think Like a Winner!* (Louisiana: Pelican Press, 1991)), 233–234.

[2] Gordon MacDonald, *Renewing Your Spiritual Passion.* (Nashville, Tenn.: Oliver-Nelson, 1989), 82.

[4] Steve Diggs, *Free to Succeed.* (Tarrytown, N.Y.: Fleming H. Revell Company, 1992), 55.

[5] Charles Swindoll, *Hand Me Another Brick.* (Nashville, Tenn.: Thomas Nelson, 1978), 84.

[6] Harriet B. Braiker, *Lethal Lovers and Poisonous People.* (New York: Pocket Books, 1992), 15.

[7] Marilyn Ferguson, *The Aquarian Conspiracy: Personal and Social Transformation in the 1980s.* (Los Angeles: J.P. Tarcher, 1980), 112.

[8] John Maxwell, *Be All You Can Be.* (Wheaton Ill.: Victor Books, 1987), 121.

[9] Alan Loy McGinnis, *The Friendship Factor.* (Minneapolis: Augsburg Press, 1979), 154.

[10] John Maxwell, *Your Attitude: Key To Success.* (San Bernardino, Calif., Here's Life Publishers), 62.

[11] Steve Diggs, op. cit., 55.

[12] Charles Swindoll, *Strengthening Your Grip.* (Waco, Tex.: Word Books, 1982), 206.

[13] Quoted in John Powell, *Happiness is an Inside Job.* (Allen, Tex.: Tabor Publishing, 1989), 27.

[14] Les Brown, *Live Your Dreams.* (New York: William Morrow and Company, Inc., 1992), 200.

[15] Braiker, op. cit., 245.

CHAPTER ELEVEN

BALANCING YOUR RELATIONAL DEMANDS

At the end of your life, you will never regret not having passed one more test, not winning one more verdict or not closing one more deal. You will regret time not spent with a husband, a friend, a child or a parent.

FORMER U. S. FIRST LADY BARBARA BUSH

A letter to Joyce Lain Kennedy, an advice columnist in the Dallas morning news, read, "I'm forty-three, a successful professional still on my way up and unhappy. With my long hours, I sometimes feel that I'm running between the raindrops. My personal life has been a series of exploding relationships, including one divorce. I feel successful on the highway of life, but I'm not driving the scenic route."[1]

One-Dimensional People

Tragically we are discovering more and more people whose competence is limited to the workplace. Bob Shank, in his dealings with people in the business world, has observed, "There comes a traumatic moment when they have to leave the office and re-enter real life. The prominence they enjoyed in the market is about to be replaced by an intense sense of dysfunction. Their contemporaries tell them they are successful, but privately they admit their capability ends at the business door."[2] We need to cultivate healthy relationships with people outside the workplace for the purpose of mutual edification. When our careers dominate our time and energy, neglected personal relationships become increasingly unsatisfying. We fall prey to the tendency to overperform in our career and underperform in all other roles, and as a result we are in danger of becoming one-dimensional beings.

With all the various roles you have to fill as parent, spouse, friend, employee, mentor and church leader, you may feel pulled in too many directions. There just doesn't seem to be enough time to do everything. "One of the crucial adjustments," says sociologist Michael Zey, "is learning how to balance commitment to career against commitment to family, to manage the standard conflict between public and private obligations."[3] We have all known individuals who could not determine what the balance should be. Divorce courts are full of people who, having thrown themselves into success at their work, found out they were something less than successful at the things that matter most. Yankelovich Clancy Shuhnan, a research firm that conducts an annual survey on American values and lifestyles, reported in 1990 that both men and women are beginning to reassess the trade-offs between work and family. "They questioned the priorities and values by which they had been living and came to a new realization of the importance of the nonwork spheres of their lives."[4] Having a successful career and a fulfilling personal life demands that we become multi-dimensional. Studies indicate those who maintain a balanced approach to work, family, friendships, play and self are more likely to be happy in life and effective in their work roles.[5] Joan Kofodimos has done some fascinating studies on the work and life challenges of managers and executives. She indicates that there is a renewed interest in the cultivation of relational networks for successful businessmen.

> In part, these changing values and needs may represent a historical pendulum swing away from the emphasis on ambition, achievement, and financial success prevalent in the 1980s. In that decade, according to historians, the gradual loss of leisure that had been occurring in the American middle class over the prior two decades reached its most extreme point. It may be that participants in the work-and-success frenzy of the 1980s found that the single minded pursuit of success did not deliver the fulfillment it promised.[7] People are wanting "a satisfying, healthy, and productive life that includes work, play and love; that integrates a range of activities with attention to self and to

personal and spiritual development; and that expresses a person's unique wishes, interests, and values."[8]

How does it happen that people who have demonstrated the talent, commitment, and willpower to climb an organization's hierarchy and to run multi-million-dollar operations seem unable to develop the skills they need to take charge of their relationships? Whatever the reason, taking charge and creating balance in our lives is never easy.[9] However, *no amount of success at the office can compensate for failure at home.*

Some people, in an attempt to cope with the realities of pressure in the '90s, are "cashing out," says futurist Faith Popcorn. No longer wanting to put up with the frenzied schedule that controls them, people are questioning their career and personal satisfaction and are opting out for a simpler lifestyle.[10] But cashing out and moving to a farm in Montana may not be a realistic option for most people. Nor should it be. For most of us achieving balance in life is a more realistic objective.

"Creating balance does not involve following a standard recipe for devoting equal amounts of time and energy to work and to personal life. Rather, balance involves finding the allocation of time and energy that fits your values and needs, making conscious choices about how to structure your life, and integrating inner needs and outer demands. Balance involves the ability to express, and experience rewards from expressing, both masterful and intimate sides of one's self. And it involves honoring and living by your deepest personal qualities, values, and goals."[11]

How can I attempt to arrange my relational world, with its demands on my limited time and energy, when I can't keep up with the commitments I've already made?

Priority Management

Few of the really valuable things in life happen by chance. People make them a priority and focus their time and energy to make them happen. Author Peter Senge makes the following suggestions for enhancing one's nonwork spheres:

- Identify what is truly important to you.
- Make a choice (commitment).
- Be truthful with those around you regarding your choice.

- Do not try to manipulate them into agreement or superficial support.[12]

It really comes down to priorities. This chapter is not about time management, because we cannot manage time. All we can do is manage our priorities. The connection between work and nonwork spheres of our lives is not a conflict over time, but over priorities.

The Law of Limited Resources

"More energy put into work implies less energy available for other areas, such as marriage, children, friendships, or outside interests such as ministry. Researchers have found, for example, that many successful executives and managers are more career-oriented and less family-oriented than their less successful colleagues. Managers focused on work life turned their attention away from their families; the family's needs are given low priority as job and workplace become increasingly central. Such managers tend to lose touch with other aspects of life as well. It is no surprise that when managers' occupational demands increase, their marital and life satisfaction decreases."[13]

The *Wall Street Journal* reported in July 1991 that more than 60 percent of respondents from Fortune 500 corporations said their jobs "robbed them of adequate energy and time to do things with their families."[14] What many CEOs don't understand is that work and family are intricately intertwined; if a leader isn't overworked, and his family life is in balance, the leader will be a more happier, more productive employee.

How Can I Change?

Larry Wilson, founder and director of Pecos River Learning Center in Santa Fe, New Mexico, says there are three ways people change. "The first is through shock. You get a divorce, you lose your job, you have a heart attack. The shock wakes you up. Another way people change is through evolution. You look around and see everyone else is changing and think that maybe you can do it too. We call this adapting. There are costs connected with both those kinds of change. The cost of a heart attack is obvious, and the cost of evolutionary change is the amount of opportunity lost. "The third way people change is through anticipation. You go out, take a look around, create a vision, come back and decide something is different than it is. That's the creative or strategic process."[15]

Andrew Ackermann, at one time director of a major consulting firm, found that his job demanded a large amount of time on the road. With his high absenteeism the joke around his house when he got home was that his kids should be sure to wear their name tags. But while recovering from a coronary he began to question his priorities. He began asking himself the question, "Why does the price of success include giving up family life, when your family is the reason you're working so hard?"[16]

Ackermann decided to "re-engineer his life. He scaled back significantly his hours at work, attended Yale's divinity school, and became a deacon in an Episcopal church. His approach to achieving balance was as follows: "Make sure the need for money doesn't cheat you out of less measurable forms of success. At work, establish the limits of what you will and will not do, and then defend them. The best companies are anxious to respond."[17]

Unfortunately, too many people wait till a crisis before they do anything about their relational priorities. Like the old adage, "You don't know what you have until it's gone," they strive for success on one road, only to discover what they really want is on another path. Managers and executives who have experienced a crisis, and consequently have realigned their priorities and commitments, have had to renounce some of their ambition and disinvest in their careers in order to begin the work of repairing their personal lives.[18]

Maybe you are looking at life after a crisis, and in light of that you want to prioritize. It is not uncommon for people to re-evaluate the path their lives are taking. Maybe you are seeing the changes that are going on in your family and you don't like what you see. Maybe you are becoming aware of the tremendous advantage people have who have deliberately given attention to their relational environment. Maybe you have come to the point in your personal reflection that you are deciding to adjust your priorities and give greater time and energy to your constellation of dynamic relationships. How do you go about instituting change?

Obviously, the first step toward constructive change is *dissatisfaction with your current life state.* There is a sense of discrepancy between the kind of life you have now and the kind you want to have. Old patterns of relating are difficult to break, but not impossible. One has to recognize that the phenomenon of inertia makes it simply easier to go on as we have been.

The second step in the change process is to *assess your situation.* What areas of your life are already strong? What relationships need to be added? Which ones need to be minimized? Are there some important relationships that have been so neglected that nothing more than a total transformation will revive them?

Restoring the Balance

Demonstrate your commitment to relationships by how you schedule your time. You set priorities in your professional arena, why not set them in your personal life?

As a pastor I have spent time with people in the last days and hours of their lives here on earth. In reflecting on their lives, I have never heard anyone say, 'I wish I had spent more time at the office." I have often heard people say, 'I wish I hadn't taken life so seriously" or "I wish I had given more attention to my spouse." In many respects where you spend your time indicates your level of commitment, your goals, and your desire to connect with significant others in your life.

In today's language we speak in terms of time management, but really it is priority management. As management consultant Harold Taylor notes, "All we can ever hope to do is manage ourselves with respect to time."[19]

Harold Taylor, in his excellent little book *Make Time Work for You,* discusses the concept of advance decision making. He suggests that we should plan our calendars ahead of the clock. In other words determine your priorities and place them into your calendar. In the same way you create a budget to clarify your priorities with respect to their money, you need to determine your time priorities in a way that reflects your relational goals. By placing priority items into your calendar, you are attempting to make certain that what you say are your priorities actually get the time they deserve.

Author and business consultant Stephen Covey, in his book *First Things First,* relates the following illustration. 'I attended a seminar once where the instructor was lecturing on time. At one point, he said, 'Okay, it's time for a quiz.' He reached under the table and pulled out a wide-mouth gallon jar. He set it on the table next to a platter with some fist-sized rocks on it. 'How many of theses rocks do you think we can get in the jar?' he asked.

"After we made our guess, he said, 'Okay. Let's find out.' He set one rock in the jar…then another…then another. I don't remember how many he got in, but he got the jar full. Then he asked, 'Is the jar full?' Everyone looked at the rocks and said 'Yes.'

"Then he said, 'Ahhh.' He reached under the table and pulled out a bucket of gravel. Then he dumped some gravel in and shook the jar, and the gravel went in all the little spaces left by the big rocks. Then he grinned and said once more, 'Is the jar full?' By this time we were on to him. 'Probably not,' we said.

"'Good!' he replied. And he reached under the table and brought out a bucket of sand. He started dumping the sand in and it went in all the little spaces left by the rocks and the gravel. Once more he looked at us and said, 'Is the jar full?'

"'No!' we all roared. He said, 'Good!' and he grabbed a pitcher of water and began to pour it in. He got something like a quart of water in that jar. Then he said, 'Well, what's the point?' Someone said, 'Well, there are gaps, and if you really work at it, you can always fit more into your life.'

"'No,' he said, 'that's not the point. The point is this: If you hadn't put these big rocks in first, would you ever have gotten any of them in?'"[20] With advanced decision making we determine what our priorities are, then we allow the other aspects of our lives to flow in and around them. It is important that those big priorities get into our calendar—your family, your spouse, your ministry commitments. Planning life rather than simply letting it just happen is imperative to someone who wants to restore balance to life.

Emotional Focus

Discipline of your time is not the only prerequisite in seeking to balance professional and personal relationships. You must also begin to focus your energies toward the people with whom you want to have a relationship. You see, time is not the only issue that people have to deal with in maintaining a balance; energy is also an issue. One person wrestling with the issue of balancing home and work life shares this story:

> I was on a holiday when I first noticed (or at least chose to acknowledge) that I wasn't doing a good job of balancing my home and work life. Like most businessmen, I got a tremendous amount of satisfaction, despite the pressure and vast number of changes that were occurring in my organization, from my work world. Goals and objectives were clear, and when you achieve something in the work world it's rewarded almost instantly, or at least the reward is obvious.
>
> One of my three children commented as we were walking down the beach that it was really nice to have me around for a change and to spend time with me.
>
> "We never to get talk, dad. We never do anything," he said.
>
> I started to object, feeling a little defensive. "What do you mean, we never... why, just last week, didn't we throw a ball around?"
>
> "No, Dad, that wasn't last week. That was three weeks ago."
>
> Three weeks ago, I thought. I began to observe how much time I spent in my inner world dealing with work-related material. There was a tremendous management inequity. About 90 percent of my skills were applied to my work and, at best, 10 percent to home life. I observed that I was much better at listening to and giving people time in my work world than I was at my home. The pressures from work had begun to invade my home life. Even before I left the house in the morning, I was already mentally at work, and I was still mentally at work when I arrived home in the evening.[21]

Restoring relational balance involves giving our relational network, particular our family, quality time, not left-over time. Many leaders confess to "Giving his best to work, but feeling too drained to give more to the family. After spending the day being composed, in control, and in charge, the person might see home as an outlet for venting suppressed frustrations from the day, or a place where it is safe to relax the self monitoring and diplomatic behavior required at work."[22]

This may explain in part how we have the propensity to be kinder to the people that we work with than the people who we are closest to. If we started reacting to our boss the way we react to our spouse, or treat our friends in the way we treat our parents, we could very well be unemployed and friendless.

Nadine Stair, in reflecting upon her eighty-five years, penned these words regarding priorities:

I'd dare to make more mistakes next time.
I'd relax. I would limber up.
I would be sillier than I have been this trip.
I would take fewer things seriously.
I would take more chances.
I would take more trips.
I would climb more mountains and swim more rivers.
I would eat more ice cream and less beans.
I would perhaps have more actual troubles
    but I'd have fewer imaginary ones.
You see, I'm one of those people who live sensibly and sanely
    hour after hour, day after day.
Oh, I've had my moments and if I had it do over again,
    I'd have more of them. In fact,
    I'd try to have nothing else. Just moments.
One after another, instead of living so many years ahead
    of each day.

I've been one of those people who never go anywhere
    without a thermometer, a hot water bottle, a raincoat
    and a parachute.
If I had to do it again, I would travel lighter next time.

If I had to live my life over,
    I would start barefoot earlier in the spring
    and stay that way later in the fall.
I would go to more dances.
I would ride more merry-go-rounds.
I would pick more daisies.[23]

How do you want to be remembered? How do you want your epitaph to read? If you had it all to do over again, would you spend more time at the office? Or would you seek to build as many close, positive relationships as possible?

Action Steps

1. *Do a reality check.* On a piece of paper list what you believe to be the top ten priorities in your life. After the list is compiled take out your calendar and examine all the fifteen-minute increments of your life over the past two weeks. Does the way you spend your time reflect the priorities you have established for your life? For an even more objective evaluation, ask your spouse for feedback.

2. *Engage in advance decision-making.* Put your priority items into your calendar. Become proactive—who are the people you need to be spending time with? Who would you like to learn from? Who would you like to teach? Who needs you? Who do you need? By placing your priorities right into your planner and allowing the other items to flow in and around them, you can a systematically limit less important items.

3. *Maximize the time you have.* Where you are is where you are. Perhaps you need to make changes, or alter your lifestyle, but there are probably some things you could do right now to improve your relational network. To give the people in your network quality time when you are fresh, alert, and at your best requires a tremendous amount of self-control. To make the necessary changes to your life so that you can develop relationships requires even more. But nothing else will leave a legacy; nothing else will impact your life more.

Notes

[1] Philip Earnest Johnson, *Time Out! Restoring Your Passion for Life, Love and Work.* (Toronto: Stoddart Publishing Co., 1992), 57.

[2] Bob Shank, *Total Life Management.* (Portland, Oreg.: Multnomah Press, 1990), 14

[3] Michael Zey, *The Mentor Connection.* (New Brunswick, N.J.: Transaction Publishers, 1990)

⁴ Joan Kofodimos, *Balancing Act: How Managers can Integrate Successful Careers and Fulfilling Personal Lives.* (San Francisco: Jossey-Bass, 1993), 2.

⁵ Ibid, 8.

⁶ Peter M. Senge, *The Fifth Discipline: The Art and Practice of the Learning Organization.* (New York: Doubleday Currency, 1990), 307.

⁷ Kofodimos, op. cit., 2–3.

⁸ Ibid, xiii.

⁹ Ibid, 3.

¹⁰ Faith Popcorn, *The Popcorn Report.* (New York: Harper Business, 1992), 190.

¹¹ Kofodimos, op. cit., 8.

¹² Senge, op. cit., 310.

¹³ Kofodimos, op. cit., 29.

¹⁴ Greg Johnson and Mike Yorkey. Daddy's Home: *A Practical Guide for Maximizing the Most Important Hours of Your Day.* (Wheaton, Ill.: Tyndale Publishers, 1992), 23.

¹⁵ Jay Conger, *Learning to Lead.* (San Francisco: Jossey-Bass, 1992), 58.

¹⁶ Sherman, Stratford. "Leaders Learn to Heed the Voice Within," in *Fortune,* 22 August 1994, 100.

¹⁷ Ibid, 100.

¹⁸ Kofodimos, op. cit., 36

¹⁹ Harold Taylor, *Making Time Work for You: A Guide Book to Effective and Productive Time Management.* (Toronto: General Publishing Co., 1981) 19.

²⁰ Stephen R Covey, A. Roger Merrill and Rebecca R. Merrill, *First Things First.* (New York: Simon and Shuster, 1994) 88–89.

²¹ Peter Jensen, *The Inside Edge: High Performance Through Mental Fitness.* (Toronto, Ont.: Macmillan Canada, 1992) 21.

²² Kofodimos, op.cit., 30.

²³ Nadine Stair, "If I Had My Life to Live Over", in *Chicken Soup for the Soul.* (Deerfield, Fla.: Health Communications, 1993), 287–288. This poem which has been passed around and reprinted for years, has been attributed to Nadine Stair. The general consensus is that she wrote the poem at age eighty-five while living in Kentucky. We have been unable to contact any family member to verify these claims.